ALWAYS AGAIN

NEW WORK FROM THE PHILIPPINES AND PHILIPPINE DIASPORAS

T0387371

LAUREL FLORES FANTAUZZO
GUEST EDITOR

S. SHANKAR
SERIES EDITOR

Mānoa: A Pacific Journal of International Writing

Series Editor
S. Shankar

Managing Editor
Amanda Galvan Huynh

Advisory Board
Joseph Han
Kristiana Kahakauwila
Emily Jungmin Yoon
Noʻu Revilla

Editorial Interns
Carson Campos
Alexa Cho
Gabriella Contratto

Corresponding Editors for Asia and the Pacific
CAMBODIA   Sharon May, Christophe Macquet, Trent Walker
CHINA   Chen Zeping, Karen Gernant, Ming Di
HONG KONG   Shirley Geok-lin Lim
INDONESIA   John H. McGlynn
JAPAN   Leza Lowitz
KOREA   Bruce Fulton
NEW ZEALAND AND SOUTH PACIFIC   Vilsoni Hereniko, Alexander Mawyer
PACIFIC LATIN AMERICA   Noah Perales-Estoesta
PHILIPPINES   Alfred A. Yuson
SOUTH ASIA   Alok Bhalla, Sukrita Paul Kumar
WESTERN CANADA   Trevor Carolan

CONTENTS

Editor's Note

It has been many years since *Mānoa* showcased contemporary literature from the Philippines and its extensive diaspora. *Always Again*, ably curated by Laurel Flores Fantauzzo, award-winning writer extraordinaire of fiction and nonfiction, remedies that oversight. The stunning works gathered here—an evocative novel excerpt, a powerful poem fashioned out of found language, lyrical translations, potent personal testimonies, insightful essayistic explorations, surreal stories that bend the line between fact and fiction, and more, much more—demonstrate the continuing vitality of writing from the Philippines and its diaspora.

An American reader might view these works from the vantage point of the particular relationship of the Philippines to the United States, but to my mind, the voices gathered here are both distinctive and essential for what they add to a larger global literary conversation—for how they show that true works of literature can wring powerful insights both from extraordinary situations of exile and dictatorship and from ordinary conditions of everyday life. These works should resonate far and wide.

Before I leave you to the pleasures and lessons of *Always Again*, a few announcements and acknowledgments.

Let me first direct you to *Mānoa*'s revamped website, which you can find at manoajournal.org, and especially to its blog, where you will find interviews, reviews, and more. We hope to make this blog a lively space for literary conversation. Feel free to contact us via the website if you would like to pitch us an idea for the blog.

With this issue, we welcome Joseph Han to the Editorial Board. Joseph has a special interest in Korea and its diaspora and the literature of Hawaiʻi, and he is the author of the celebrated novel *Nuclear Family*. We look forward to working with him in the years to come. Audrey Beaton, Anna Kalabukhova, and Chandanie Somwaru—the three interns at the journal—continued as part of the *Mānoa* team till the end of the Spring 2024 semester; and Carson Campos, Alexa Cho, and Gabriella Contratto came on board as the three new interns at the start of Fall 2024 semester. They made valuable and multifaceted contributions to the journal.

We gratefully acknowledge awards from the Amazon Literary Partnership Literary Magazine Fund and the Community of Literary Magazines and Presses, as well as from the Center for Philippine Studies at the University of Hawai'i at Mānoa, for support that made the publication of this issue possible.

S. Shankar
Honolulu, Hawai'i

Guest Editor's Introduction: On This Gathering_____

In this guest editor's introduction, I must make two confessions.

The first confession, "Always Again," the title of this collection, began as a phrase I used in bitterness.

I'm Filipina American—an Italiapina, as my friends say—or Filipinx, in the ongoing lexicon of how we of the Philippine diaspora refer to ourselves. I came of age traveling back and forth between the United States and the Philippines, starting with a journey to Manila with my mother when I was twelve. I lived in Metro Manila as a teacher and a writer in my twenties and thirties, and now I travel from Los Angeles, one of the capitals of the Philippine American diaspora, to Metro Manila for month-long visits.

I have been fortunate to be of two countries and to have the material and temporal capacity to inhabit both. So it is not the healthiest urge, I realize, to begin with bitterness.

But "always again" is the reversal of that aspirational phrase, "never again." Never again to atrocity and dictatorship. Never again to the horrors leaders can visit upon a people.

I thought of the phrase "always again" when Rodrigo Roa Duterte won the 2016 elections. I stayed up all night on a friend's couch, wondering who would survive and who would die during Duterte's brutal regime.

After all the violence and impunity of that reign, I thought, "Always again," in the run-up to the 2022 elections in the Philippines, when journalist friends told me they observed a solid majority in favor of electing Ferdinand "Bong Bong" Marcos, Jr. When Bong Bong did win, beating out the human rights attorney candidate with no record of corruption, I thought the phrase again. Always again, the country's worst political families proceed like zombies, feeding on viral and social media lies and citizens' ennui. Again, the unrepentant family of the unrepentant plunderer—the original human rights violating diktador, Ferdinand Marcos, Sr.—runs the country.

Always again, typhoons return, stronger and faster, taking our most vulnerable peoples into their winds and waters. Cycles of classist and imperialist impunities repeat with the quiet rhythm of mundane evil. Immigration, with all its attendant loneliness and hardship, continues out of the archipelago; my own family departed for California in the late 1970s, during the horrors of the first Marcos regime.

And yet.

Always again, joy, community, and thriving take place alongside the natural and unnatural extremes of what the people of the Philippines suffer. In Manila, gardens grow in the harshest asphalted climates, shoots reaching brilliantly green from buckets, plastic bottles, and old shoes. Activists and the rarest of civic workers move into the breaches left by leaders who betray us, forming oases of resistance, healthy demands, and mutual care. Children find ways to play in every kind of street and waterway. The youth remind us, as our cover does, to look to the stars in great darkness. As much as suffering repeats, so does a powerful legacy of resistance.

Bitterness is the shortest, most incomplete story. No single narrative—like no single language—rules the Philippines or its diasporas. The islands and their climates form archipelagos of deep contradictions and shape a people of persistent laughter. There is no party like a Philippine party, no daily hangouts more epic than those that celebrate the everyday miracle of survival. Even with the sparsest ingredients, Filipinos will find a way to feast.

That's how I choose to see this collection: as a rich gathering. A reveling in what words and images can do to preserve, to resurrect, to celebrate, and to create, even in the most difficult conditions.

And here I must make my second confession. Always, again, I think of my friends who died.

I do so with great affection and unsolvable longing, my mind going to the ones with whom I'd most like to share what I have curated here. If we are lucky enough to age, I suppose it is our destiny to have our gaze go to that audience: to the ones who have gone before us to that place we all will eventually go.

Over my twenties and thirties, I gathered friends and mentors—or, I should say, friends and mentors gathered me. They shared with me, over the years, their deep knowledge of the Philippines. My teachers were Susan Quimpo, an author, educator, and activist against dictatorship; Gayia Gesite Beyer, an anthropologist and a guide to Banaue, in the mountainous north of the Philippines, her indigenous home; and Ged Hidalgo, a teacher of young children, a visual artist, and a musician who played indigenous instruments from many regions of the archipelago. The three of them did not live to see the end of the awful pandemic lockdown in the Philippines. But they live on in me, in so many other loved ones, and in the communities they reached. And so I dedicate this issue to them, and I offer it to you, too.

I hope the work that gathers here teaches readers well—as well as my friends and mentors taught me.

Laurel Flores Fantauzzo
Historic Filipinotown, Los Angeles, California

We open class with still images where———————————

by the thousands above Costa Brava
starlings flock and tumble, swirl in answer

to some unseen danger, their looping dark
against that bonfire sky, shifting: a
haze of wings and panicked rally cries, a
spiral galaxy, bodies together

becoming chorus, then a shadow bird
my students say reminds them of tidal
pools or smoke, the states of matter. I spell

murmuration and listen as they write
murder in their notes instead. It is May.

We are not safe. But we'll go when drill bells
sound—will play invisible, cut our lights,
shut the blinds, block every way out and wait.

Crab Mentality

The noodle dish I associate
with an avenue. A memory
of feeling the building sway

and gazing at the shapes of
people in prayer as the earth
shook. Iridescent orange orbs

of fat on a bed of fragility.
I, too, pray: I would like to
remain. I love my country,

the sea that resaturates
it. I liken myself to lámbay
from Bantáyan among other

kinds of crabs, numerous and
teetering. A skyline at hightide.
What if I make it out alive?

What then? I love my countrymen
except when I shouldn't. To survive
is the secret recipe, so I must.

Be Kind, Rewind

Cherry Court, ancestor
of the mall, with a shop
that sold baking supplies
and flowers we could eat.
Next door, a video store.
My sister and I need to watch
The Land Before Time again.
Again we choose to watch
the mother die, rewinding
to her mortal wound, the leaf
she left behind. Littlefoot's loss
is ours for now. The Tree Star
appears delicious. The promise
of the Great Valley lessens
our grief, a word we're only
starting to learn. The Mysterious
Beyond. Later, in another faraway
country, I am told the problem
with loving a thing too much
is the need to own it. When I return
to that archway, those pink betamax
days, I taste an innocence like sugar.
Now, I keep an inventory of fears,
like earthquakes or unexpected
turbulence. The further I go back,
the braver I feel. Oh, I was so brave.

*We're Always Thinking about Our Dead*_____

The TV turned itself off, then on,
then off again. Light bulbs flickering.
A voice called out: *inday!* Inday
is what they used to call her.

Two months after the typhoon,
we visit their graves.
We're sorry it took this long.
There was a typhoon.

We received your message.
We learned from the group chat
that your souls paid us a visit.
Breaking news: we're OK.

We want to know
if there's ube ice cream
where you are. If heaven
is eating a banana a day

and laughing together
at the same silly jokes.
We've kept this routine
going: the larger the moth,

the deeper the prayer.
The larger the moth, the more
we remember to remember.
The whole science of it.

The hardest part comes after
the after. The question of who
will bring the tables and the chairs.
A question of who will be there.

Wife————————————————————————

her aberrant behavior

her abnormal or pathological lies

her abuse

her admission to an affair

her adultery

her alleged singing career

her arrest in Japan due to overstaying

her beauty

her being a model in her early life

her being the breadwinner of the family

her choosing to work in a nightclub instead of engaging in a decent job

her coldly treating her husband, verbally and sexually

her constant mahjong sessions

her current psychological state

her disregard for the rights of others

her dysfunctional family

her exhibited insecurities

her extreme jealousy

her extreme perversion and depravity

her family background

her father's death in a vehicular accident when she was in her teens

her formative years

her frequent partying with friends

her gambling

her highly unusual acts

her histrionic personality disorder

her inability to assume the essential marital obligations

her inability to discharge her marital obligations

her inability to understand and perform the essential obligations of marriage

her insensitivity toward her husband's feelings

her intolerance of the conventional behavioral limitations imposed by society

her invented personalities and situations

her letters using fictitious names

her low tolerance for boredom

her mahjong sessions

her maladaptive behavior

her mistreatment and control of others without remorse

her moral bankruptcy

her Narcissistic Personality Disorder

her neglect of parental duties

her neglect of their children

her night life with friends

her obsessive need for attention from other men

her obvious failure to fully appreciate the duties and responsibilities of parenthood

her own childhood experience

her own mother

her partying ways

her perennially telling lies

her persistence

her persistent lying

her personality

her poor upbringing

her quick anger at the slightest provocation or for no reason

her ridiculous stories

her self-indulgence

her several boyfriends

her singing abilities

her state of health

her tendency to blame others

her threats of blackmail and of committing suicide

her threats of leaving if her ideas are not agreed to

her unabashed declaration of having no feelings for her husband

her unawareness of her disorder

her visits to the beauty parlor

her wanton disregard

her whims

her whole lifestyle

her world of make-believe

is a different person

is a heavy smoker

is a result of childhood trauma and defective child-rearing practices

is afflicted by histrionic personality disorder

is always a bit lonely

is apt to be a dependent person

is assertive when opinions contrary to those of her own are expressed

is clingy and immature

is constantly demanding reassurance

is doubting his love

is easily influenced by friends

is emotionally immature

is extremely exploitative and aggressive

is fond of her group of friends

is going out of the house without his permission

is grave, permanent and incurable

is hard-headed

is highly impressionable

is impulsive and domineering

is irritable

is lacking in analytical ability

is likely to be reserved

is markedly antithetical to the substantive content and implications of
the Marriage Covenant

is more fond of friends than family

is perceived by others as selfish, egotistical and unreliable

is reckless and without consideration of his feelings

is seemingly detached in her ways

is self-centered and narcissistic

is self-centered to the point of neglecting her duty as a wife and as a mother

is selfish and egotistical

is so concerned with herself in her own lifestyle

is somewhat exploitative

is still egocentrically involved with herself

is suffering from histrionic personality disorder

is suffering from a Histrionic Personality Disorder with Narcissistic
Features

is suffering the grave, severe, and incurable presence of Narcissistic and Antisocial Personality Disorder

is suggestible

is truly incognitive of her marital responsibilities

is unable to distinguish between fantasy and reality

is unconscious of her personality disorder

is undoubtedly in the wreck and weakly founded

is unlawful, insincere and undoubtedly uncaring in her strides toward convenience

is unmoved by his persistence

is upset when she cannot get what she wants

that a cure thereof would be a remarkable feat

that her avowals as to her commitment to the marriage cannot be accorded much credence

that her condition is incurable

that her psychosis is quite grave

that her uncle also showed him his guns

that it became an obsession

that it began to inflate her ego

that it continued until adulthood

that it is grave

that it is narcissism where the person falls in love with himself

that it started during her adolescence

that it started since childhood and only manifested during marriage that no such occasion had taken place

that not a single member of her family ever witnessed

that one instance of sexual infidelity

that paranoid jealousy

that pathological liar

that she acted irrationally

that she actually wanted to get out of their lives

that she admitted the truth in one of their quarrels

that she altered her payslip to make it appear that she earned a higher income

that she always challenged his opinions on what he thinks is proper

that she appeared to be dating other men

that she bought a sala set from a public market but told him she acquired it from a famous furniture dealer

that she brought her children with her to her mahjong sessions

that she came from a fine family despite having a lazy father

that she cannot delay to gratify her needs

that she cannot stand disappointment

that she cannot stand frustration

that she caused him such stress that he was hospitalized

that she chose to walk away from their marriage

that she claimed to be a singer or a freelance voice talent

that she cohabited with her lover

that she concealed the fact that she previously gave birth

that she confessed her romantic affair with a Japanese man

that she confronted him as to why he appeared to be cold

that she continued to lie, fabricate stories, and maintain her excessive jealousy

that she continued working in a Manila nightclub

that she could ignore or threaten to accede to her desires

that she could not appreciate or absorb or fulfill the obligations of marriage which everybody takes for granted

that she demands immediate gratification

that she despised advice or suggestion from her elders

that she did not end the illicit relationship

that she displays her feelings openly and freely

that she ended up borrowing money from other people on false pretexts

that she fabricated a story about her brother-in-law

that she fabricated friends

that she fears that others will abandon her

that she had an affair with a Japanese national

that she had been afflicted with Narcissistic Personality Disorder as well as with Antisocial Disorder

that she had "compulsive and dependent tendencies"

that she had her own priorities

that she herself never experienced the care and affection of her own mother that she introduced her husband as her brother to her Japanese lover

that she introduced the boy as the adopted child of her family

that she invented friends named Babes Santos and Via Marquez

that she kept him in the dark about her natural child's real parentage

that she kept on telephoning him

that she let her Japanese boyfriend visit the conjugal home

that she likes to be around people

that she likes to play mahjong a lot

that she likewise refused to have sexual intercourse

that she loves to fabricate about herself

that she made up letters from fictitious characters

that she may appear critical and demanding

that she may keep her emotional distance

that she may not be that demonstrative of her affections

that she misrepresented herself as a psychiatrist to her obstetrician

that she obtained high scores on dependency, narcissism and compulsiveness

that she openly had extramarital affairs

that she overreacts to even minor provocations

that she placed an enormous value on having significant others

that she preferred to work at a nightclub over a decent business offered to her

that she purchased the boat ticket

that she refused the idea

that she refused to allow him to go home

that she refused to live with him

that she represented herself as a person of greater means

that she sent lengthy letters touting herself as the "number one
moneymaker" in the commercial industry

that she shared intimate sexual moments with her boyfriend prior

that she spent lavishly on unnecessary items

that she started getting angry at him for no reason

that she started giving him the cold treatment

that she stops harassing the home of his parents

that she stops tormenting him

that she surprisingly retorted that she also hates her family

that she threatened in so many ways

that she threatened to commit suicide

that she threatened to file a case

that she told some of her friends that she graduated with a degree in
psychology

that she, too, values her relationship

that she tries to maintain a certain distance to minimize opportunities
for rejection

that she undermined the basic relationship that should be based on love,
trust and respect

that she used force and threats knowing that her husband is somehow
weak-willed

that she was a model at Hyatt and then Rustan's

that she was worth P2 million

that she would deny it to avoid criticism

that she would jump from one boyfriend to another

that she would rebel when her demands were not met

that she would similarly be unable to comprehend the legal nature of the
marital bond

the ability to adhere to the truth

the actual cases of neglect of her family

the actual manifestations of her histrionic personality disorder

the adolescent stage of her life

the adverse action and reaction pattern

the aggressive-rebellious type of woman

the attention seeking

the basic obligations of marriage

the blatant insensitivity

the breakdown of their marriage

the charade

the concessions given her

the corporal punishment to instill discipline

the corresponding obligations

the course of her marriage

the discretionary faculty impaired in its practico-concrete judgment formation

the essential marital obligations

the excessive emotionality

the extent of calling up his officemates to monitor his whereabouts

the fact when the father died

the failure of her marriage

the failure to distinguish truth from fiction, or at least abide by the truth

the fantastic ability to invent and fabricate stories and personalities

the figments of her imagination

the following indicators of her disorder

the gratification of her own personal and escapist desires

the grave and serious act

the gravity of her disorder

the gravity of her psychological incapacity

the immaturity and irresponsibility

the importance of which seems utterly lost on her

the inability to adhere to reality

the incapacity to accept

the incapacity to fulfill

the inconsistent pattern

the insincerity of maternal care

the integrality of her matrimonial consent in terms of its deliberative
component

the inveterate pathological liar

the irregular treatment she received from her parents

the Japanese lover in their house

the joy to fury to misery to despair

the kind of deprivation

the lack of any indication that behavioral or medical therapy would play
a significant role

the lack of concern

the lack of love toward the person

the lack of regard for the sanctity of the marital bond and home

the lie

the long-term effects

the manipulable inconvenience

the marital union bereft of any mutual respect

the military friends to harm his family

the moral fiber

the narcissistic and antisocial personality disorder

the need for attention

the need for love

the needs from a deprived childhood

the obsessive mahjong playing

the pain and humiliation she callously caused him

the pathologic nature of her mistruths

the pervasive pattern of behavior

the point of paranoia

the priorities of her life

the propensity to lie about almost anything

the psychological aversion to cohabit with her husband

the sanctity of marriage and family

the second time

the serious obligations which she has ignored

the severance of their marital vinculum

the slightest provocation

the state's interest

the tendency to repeat some kind of experience or the lack of care

the threat of desertion

the unsuitable behavioral patterns

the very tender ages

the way she wanted to live her life

NOTES
The Philippines is the only country in the world (aside from the Vatican) with no divorce law. The only legal recourse is to file for annulment or declaration of nullity of marriage, a process that, by design, is long, expensive, adversarial, and ultimately inaccessible. Narratives of blame are integral to this process, which requires proof of a spouse's psychological incapacity "to comply with the essential marital obligations of marriage." "Wife" is part of an ongoing project to interrogate Philippine laws on marriage by way of poetry. This poem explores the nebulous concept of

psychological incapacity, defined in jurisprudence for the most part in largely restrictive ways, as codified in *Republic v. Court of Appeals and Molina* in 1997. The poem engages with six out of only eleven Supreme Court cases in which the petition for nullity was granted since the Family Code was enacted in 1987, as listed in *Tan-Andal v. Andal* (2021). I collected phrases from all cases pinning psychological incapacity on the wife, lightly edited some phrases for syntactical consistency, and alphabetized the entire lot. From this catalog can be gleaned the ways that wives are narrativized to the point of legal legibility for the declaration of nullity to be granted. The struggle for a divorce law continues, and I hope it is achieved in my lifetime.

Kailangan

All the women
in my family
are needed
and needle
themselves into
whatever everyone
else needs.
No one ever
announces what
is needed,
which is nothing,
needless to say.

Kalokohan

My friend's kid discovers the glory of Gloria Estefan and, when prompted by her mother's question, "Is the rhythm gonna get you?" declares, "DON'T TALK ABOUT IT!" as she waves her small arms high above her head.

If you plant one clove of garlic, it will grow into a bulb. If you plant one zucchini a summer, it will be enough.

When he wasn't working at the plant or working in his garden, my father wore his Florsheim loafers and took care to condition their black leather and make their small gold buckles shine.

My mother giggles high-pitched, like a little girl with her eyes-skyward when she tries to tell a story, so funny, so funny she can't catch her breath. I laugh, too—her laughter contagious, "So, what happened? What happened?"—until my cheeks hurt, though I haven't yet heard a plot or punchline.

Once I hiked through a jungle and climbed to the summit of a mountain and there found every houseplant my parents placed throughout the corners of my childhood: pothos, snake plant, rubber tree, purple queen, ficus, fern. *Indoor, outdoor; outdoor, in.*

A robin wakes me three mornings in a row with a BANG BANG BANG that chokes me from my sleep: its poor beak, trying to break through the windows. No, no, I say. You will hurt yourself. That reflection is you. There is no other robin here. Just you, just you. I rush the window. Raise my arms, make myself big to scare it away from itself. A monster trying to help.

Kalungkutan

makes reckless cosmologists of us all
and so we build new gods and universes,
strike bargains for epic consequences:
if I find that old notebook, I will not have
lost my memories of you; if I still manage
to keep safe the note you wrote me four-
teen years ago, it will mean I can keep you
here. If I walk into the world, looking for
you around each corner, one day
you will appear.

Pagdadalamhati

the salt thrown over the shoulder
the sand a child insists will subdue the ocean
the halving and halving of atoms
that births inexplicably
a new thing—halved
and halved in our no longer having
you nor you nor you nor you
no longer you never
again you

Pikon

        translucent   onion skin
        paper skirt
                whatever hurts
        incurred   uncured
        curdles like wasps
        unfurled from a carcass
        the meat beats
        below the dermis

Stereograph: The Bones of the Tenants Whose Burial Rental Was Not Renewed—Santa Cruz Cemetery, Manila, 1899

skull skull femur *they inspect us* radius ulna *bundok na buto* tibia *puzzles* skull sacrum *inscrutable alive* scapula coccyx *perhaps solvable dead* humerus clavicle mandible *a problem of tenancy* skull sternum *can our* femur skull *bones pay anything forward* rib skull rib tibia *could our hauntings* femur tibia mandible *be monetized* pubis ilium *these two fools* skull ischium *are not princes* tarsus skull patella *and not one* *of us a jester* vertebra tibia skull skull skull *or momento mori* fibula tibia femur *but occupancy manifest* skull pubis mandile *we have yet to return to dust* clavicle scapula *where our eyes once were* humerus skull sacrum skull *we can still gape back* femur mandible vertebra *into their empty gaze* skull sternum skull *no way to desecrate us* tibia scapula femur *further* tarsus skull skull skull skull skull skull skull skull

Inventory

femur back oxtail chicken pig milkfish tinik buto   smooth
    jagged stones river stones   stones skipping
  rivers dagat koi ponds backyard ponds
        creeks culverts lakes falls full
water lettuce waterlilies   banana leaves halaman acacia
  hyacinth   roses red   roses yellow   magnolia
balete   cattails   crape myrtle nipa Bradford pear
  bougainvillea dogwood   palm   bromeliad   puno
puso   bangus dilis lionfish milkfish clownfish angelfish ocean fish
   gold fish river fish swimming without knowing
   how to lungoy
      funeral parlors karaoke sa sala cockfights drunk fights
full flights
        bahala na sa buhay mo cigarette smoke
          cherry kept close to the throat
houses on stilts on a lake
   inside a volcano inside a lake on an island of many islands
in an ocean of oceans golden lobes   golden piercings
Cadillac gold chains
   golden globs of injection molding   UAW card carrying
Big Three paychecks Big Three pink slips muscle cars carrying car
seats
    salt and snow
    twenty to a five-room   suburban sidewalks subsumed
     by the smell of frying fish
     Romulus without Remus   born dear
from toddler-sized boxes filled here   opened there
   boxes bound back   by tape and rope
  holding in Tommy and Ralph and Nike and Hershey and Spam
     only there   atis   sukang paombong
     chico   alamang maliit

mga mukha not strangers until   magsalita or ngiti
   further back
   a bangka   an ark   islands two by two
        4000 kinds of orchids   dito
               doon

Stereograph: 24045—American Soldiers Feeding Filipino Children

Pale men turn more and more red: poor contests losing their ideals. *They* are better? They kill our parents, pen us like piglets. Opportunities—little and probable brown bouts of power, born from ghost hands' appetite for glory. Look there, humanitarian! They think we will not bite. How wrong. Brown mouth, hungry, will grow up into scouts, great loud cogs, men & women spouting lingua franca, gratitude. Whitening, brightening as bettering as what's best. Ha! Free from weak blistered skin, we hold our truths: they know not one true thing of our ripening: a price of unknown consequence. Their sport: which child hungers most? Starving in open lack, perfect photographs. Lo, progress! Mores doled, old feeding, roved emptiness, empty promise: empire's feed of benevolent assimilation. Primacy a dumb lie under our powerful crossing—these stupid lines, dirt pens whose contents will fatten, spatter so pleasing so *salamat po*. They don't know how well we know to grow candor in the dark. Downcast our eyes: bundok dugo ngipin dilim. Our fresh gums, our red teeth.

Standardization

Empire: Diaspora

    a)   Pollen: Capitalists
    b)   Gold: Honeybees
    c)   Loose Change: Chumps
    d)   Diaspora: Empire

Pamilya: Family

    a)   Love: Obligation
    b)   Boundary: Guilt
    c)   Obligation: Love
    d)   Distance: Regret

Utang na Loob: American Dream

    a)   Uncle Sam: Little Brown Brother
    b)   Province: Makati
    c)   Buhay: Patay
    d)   Typhoon: The Red Cross

Nanay: Anak

    a)   Bulaklak: Araw
    b)   Filipino: American
    c)   Hungry: Full
    d)   Anak: Nanay

Failed Self-Portraits

as Last Cigarette
as Claudia Kishi
as Half-Eaten Baguette
as Drunk Bumblebee
as Cowboy Boots
as Bamboo Shoots
as Plastic Adirondack Chair
as Never Shoulda Been Permed Hair
as Telenovela Translation
as Nope Wrong Asian
as 90s Girl Group R&B
as Little Falling Butiki

Poems of Batanes

TRANSLATED BY DORIAN S. MERINA

Translator's Note

Ivatan is traditionally an oral-based language, and throughout history, various spellings have been used to try to capture the sounds in the language. Today, there are community-based efforts underway to improve and unify the written language. Here, I have relied on the spellings used by Dr. Florentino Hornedo, Dr. Cesar A. Hidalgo (in The Cultural Dictionary of Batanes*), and, most importantly, the Laji singers themselves when they expressed a preference.*

Grateful acknowledgment again to Dr. Hornedo, as his scholarship provided guidance for the Laji translations.

NU NUNUK DU TUKON

As sung by Laji Singers Melecio Alasco and Rosita Alavado

Nu nunuk du tukon, minuhung as kadisi na,
ichapungpung diya am yaken u ñilawngan na.
Kapaytalamaran ava su avang di idaúd,
ta miyan du inayebngan na, ta miyan du inayebngan na.
Nu itañis ko am nu didiwen ko
ta nu taaw aya u suminbang diyaken,
nu maliliyak a pahung as maheheyet a riyes
u minahey niya, u minahey niya diyaken.

The nunuk tree on the hill grew tender leaves and shoots,
then suddenly its crown was broken and I was caught beneath.
Now I can no longer watch the boat in the deep sea
for I stand on the side that is hidden, on the side that is hidden.
I weep in my sorrow
for the vast ocean has made me an orphan,
the pounding sea breakers, the strong currents,
they told me of my fate, they told me this.

U ANAK NU MUNAMUN

As sung by Laji Singer Filomena Hubalde

Anu kadawudawung ku du tukun di Valungut
Dawri a dinungasungay u anak nu munamun,
Ahapen ku na siya nu masen a sahakeb,
Dahuran ku na siya du mahungtub a duyuy,
Udiyan ku na niya a payrakurakuhen
A di chu'a pavulsayi su madahmet a chirin
Du kahawahawa ku niya u kaichay nu anak nu munamun.

THE CHILD OF THE MUNAMUN

Each time I look down from the hill at Valungut
I see the child of the *munamun* swimming in the waves,
I will gather her in my finest net
and place her in the deep coconut shell,
to take her home and care for her as she grows.
I will not utter a single harsh word
and take great care not to hurt the feelings
of the child of the *munamun.*

DORIAN S. MERINA

Four Tanagas

Contributor's Note
Tanaga is a traditional Filipino form of poetry. Each poem is composed of four lines, seven syllables per line, with various end-rhyme patterns. This series, titled simply Asa, Dadwa, Tatdu, Apat (One, Two, Three, Four), is my experiment with using Ivatan poetic language in the Tanaga form.

Special thanks to Anastacia Merina for her help with key phrases in the Tanaga series.

Masalawsaw sicharaw
Malatyat 'changuriyaw,
Navuya mu u hañit?
Nadngey mu u valichit?

The day is full of wind
As a new dawn arrives,
Have you seen the brightening sky?
Have you heard the *valichit* sing?

Sumavusavung da na
U dadwa ka bayakbak,
Nu minaydak a chidat
Asa yatus vituhen.

IVATAN TANAGA: TWO

The two bayakbak trees
are flowering:
a lightning bolt flashes,
a hundred bright stars.

Maychavayavaya pa
U muyin nu taaw,
Uyud a masari pa,
Malaymay 'changuriyaw.

The ocean's face has yet to blush,
The morning deep in darkness,
A gentle breeze blows
across the land.

An mawara idawud
makuyun u kakaywan
as kan taaw du mandichud
an mawara idawud.

When the idawud wind comes
the forest trembles and shakes,
as do the deep ocean breaks,
when the idawud wind comes.

Rediscovering Roots

This project explores how the pandemic-induced tourism void became a portal for an indigenous community in the Philippines to rediscover their roots.

The T'boli, most known for a craft called "dream weaving," call Lake Sebu in Mindanao home. Despite being in the hinterlands, at the dawn of budget travel, tourists poured in to see the highland tribe's vibrant heritage and witness the women called "dream weavers"—a chosen few who can weave abaca cloth with intricate patterns that are believed to visit them in their dreams. A strong tourism industry became a potent shield against land grabbers and natural resource exploitation. Economic activity flourished. Locals learned new ways to make money outside agriculture. The T'boli became the cultural face of the region.

But all this attention came with pitfalls, too. "We lose a lot of things," said Maria Todi, a tribal leader, artist, and T'boli heritage preserver. She watched as neighbors willingly traded ancestral lands for lowland possessions they envied from visitors. Large hotels and businesses owned by outsiders sprouted all over. Traditions were slowly being sidelined as foreign religions creeped in.

Then, in 2020, the coronavirus pandemic put all this expansion to a temporary halt. The T'boli, like many indigenous peoples, were once more isolated. Their heritage was theirs alone, again.

For weaver Barbara Ofong, having their heritage for themselves meant nobody was coming to buy her weaves called "T'Nalak." She borrowed money to be able to buy basic needs.

A meter of the intricate T'Nalak cloth takes several months to make. And each week without tourists became more and more depressing.

When their audience dissipated amid the lockdowns, Todi's family suffered financially. They ran a School of Living Traditions, which doubled as a homestay for backpackers. Usually bustling with tourists witnessing T'boli music and dances, it became empty.

But the family also saw the time as an opportunity to live off the land, as their forebears did.

With the T'boli community and the Todi family, this project is an ongoing introspection into how this momentary portal to a constant past weighs with the needs of an ever-changing present.

This project was initiated with support from the National Geographic Society's COVID-19 Emergency Fund for Journalists.

Oyog with Baby, 2021, Photograph by Martin San Diego

The COVID-19 pandemic served as an "opportunity for the T'boli community to go back, as they tend to run away from their roots," said Maria "Oyog" Todi, a tribal leader, cultural worker, and educator who has dedicated her life to recording and passing down the traditions of the Indigenous T'boli in the southern Philippines. Before, her days were all about entertaining tourists in Lake Sebu who are interested in the T'boli way of life and, through earnings from tourism, teaching the younger generations the vibrant art heritage their ancestors have handed down for thousands of years. Then, in early March of 2020, the pandemic arrived, and the tourists stayed home. Finances ran dry, but Todi saw it as an opportunity to focus on the one side of the T'boli life that often gets sidelined—living off the land. "Now we've learned to value our land like our forebears have," Todi said.

Kuya with Puppy, 2021, Photograph by Martin San Diego

Oyog's family takes turns in farm duties during the first week of the harvest season in the last week of August 2021 in Lake Sebu, South Cotabato, Philippines.

Kulintang, 2021, Photograph by Martin San Diego

Oyog with Boy and Kulintang, 2021, Photograph by Martin San Diego

Oyog and her nephews make a platform using bamboo for the musical instrument Kulintang, in their family farm in Lake Sebu, South Cotabato, Philippines.

Girl with Broom, 2021, Photograph by Martin San Diego

Oyog's niece Rhea on farm duties during the first week of the harvest season in the last week of August 2021 in Lake Sebu, South Cotabato, Philippines.

Ate Harvesting Rice, 2021, Photograph by Martin San Diego

Boy and Kuya with Rice, 2021, Photograph by Martin San Diego

Hands and Rice Close-Up, 2021, Photograph by Martin San Diego

Rice and Spoon Close-Up, 2021, Photograph by Martin San Diego

Rice grain is separated from the stem with a spoon during the first week of the harvest season in the last week of August 2021 in Lake Sebu, South Cotabato, Philippines.

Boy Shaking Rice, 2021, Photograph by Martin San Diego

Oyog Smiling, 2021, Photograph by Martin San Diego

Oyog poses for a portrait wearing traditional T'boli on their family farm during the first week of the harvest season in the last days of August 2021 in Lake Sebu, South Cotabato, Philippines.

Rhea Laughing, 2021, Photograph by Martin San Diego

Oyog's niece Rhea poses for portraits wearing traditional T'boli on their family farm during the first week of the harvest season in the last days of August 2021 in Lake Sebu, South Cotabato, Philippines.

Rhea with Boys, 2021, Photograph by Martin San Diego

Rhea poses for portraits wearing traditional T'boli while her cousins watch on their family farm during the first week of the harvest season in the last days of August 2021 in Lake Sebu, South Cotabato, Philippines

Going Downhill with Basket, 2021, Photograph by Martin San Diego

Boys in Foliage, 2021, Photograph by Martin San Diego

Oyog's nephews explore a nearby water source on their family farm in the hinterlands of Lake Sebu.

Carabao in Foliage, 2021, Photograph by Martin San Diego

Manang and Laundry, 2021, Photograph by Martin San Diego

Barbara "Buwat" Ofong is a Dreamweaver in Lake Sebu, South Cotabato, Philippines. She weaves patterns from her dreams using Abaca and traditional dyes. She said the pause in tourism stressed her financially as she has come to depend on it. Many in her community have pawned their lands to survive financially. Unlike Oyog, she does not like farming. But she still hopes to buy back the land she pawned to give to her grandchildren, because it's the foundation for everything.

Manang Weaving, 2021, Photograph by Martin San Diego

Manang with Weaving Work, 2024, Photograph by Martin San Diego

Lake Sebu Landscape, 2021, Photograph by Martin San Diego

The municipality of Lake Sebu in South Cotabato, Philippines, is a protected area and the ancestral domain of the T'boli indigenous people. Tourists from all over have been drawn to its natural beauty and the indigenous T'boli's rich art heritage, gradually changing the land and its people. The COVID-19 pandemic is providing indigenous peoples of the Philippines a portal to the past: a time before the dawn of infrastructure, budget travel, and social media-inspired sightseeing. The tourism void is opening up space for them to rediscover their fading roots, but may have left them empty-handed for the needs of the present.

Lake Sebu Fishponds, 2021, Photographed by Martin San Diego

Man on Boat in Lake Sebu, 2021, Photographed by Martin San Diego

A Writer's Secret Moves: On a Paired Rereading of Rizal's Noli *and* Fili

For Benedict Anderson and my students at University of Hawai'i at Mānoa, spring 2024: Sara, Josie, Elijah, Andrew, Joe, Monica, Malia, Alex, Hiroko, and Jake, who read Rizal with me, enduring my speculations.

I'd like to talk about Rizal here from my perspective, from reading him as a maker of fiction. Jose Rizal is the Philippines' national hero, but he was also an ophthalmologist, amateur zoologist, farmer, sculptor, educator, ethnologist, and poet. However, above all, he was the Philippines' Original Gangster of a novelist.

My favorite among Rizal's works is the *Fili*—*El Filibusterismo*, his second novel, published in Ghent, Belgium, in 1891, continuing the saga of Crisostomo Ibarra, masked as Simoun, an anticlerical, anticolonial jeweler from South America (yes, Rizal went transnational in the *Fili*), who foments conspiracy and rebellion against Spain. Oddly, the *Fili* could also be called a college novel, set mostly among student activists in nineteenth-century Manila. Some of the ideas in this essay come from pen-pal conversations I once had with Benedict Anderson, the Irish scholar on Southeast Asian history and political science whose thoughts on Rizal are ground for his essential concepts on nation-making, his most famous work being the classic textbook on nationalism, *Imagined Communities*. In Rizal's novels, Ben found exemplary ground for his theories on how nations are "imagined," thus made.

So I dedicate this essay to Ben—Om Ben, as he liked to be called.

I used to pose theories to Ben on Rizal as an artist, mostly for fun, to get him to think along with me (we had diametrically opposite tastes in fiction; he preferred realism). Ben and I bonded (in our letters; I met him only once) over what turned out to be our shared love for the *Fili*. Unlike Ben, I was not so much a lover of Rizal's first novel, *Noli Me Tangere*, which helped inspire revolution against Spain; it's the Philippines' (and nation-making's) *ur*-novel. But no one I knew could move with me into my nerdy *Fili*-love as Benedict Anderson could.

Disclaimer: I love Rizal. He's a mutant nerd before whom my irony fails. It's not just that Rizal spoke at least a dozen languages—including Tagalog, Cebuano, Cavite-Chabacano, English, French, Italian, German, and of course Spanish (though not including my own, Waray); wrote realist yet also mysteriously playful novels; and blazed a trail on narrative art that is important to the world, not just the Philippines. Most importantly, he had an uncanny and undaunted self-regard—he centered himself and his country—at a time when the Spanish colonial Philippines was in dire straits. It's important to note that at one point in Rizal's time, the Philippines was ruled by the man who, during the Spanish-American War, was known as the Butcher of Havana, or just "Butcher," Governor-General Valeriano Weyler—though Weyler was only one among many insensible rulers of the Philippines, then and now. Rizal was sui generis, and we're lucky as Filipinos to have him, period.

So I'm not one who'd like to smash the idol with my hip wit—that's a job equally entertaining for some other reader, or maybe some other me. For this rereading project, I read first chapter 1 of the *Fili*, then chapter 1 of the *Noli*, and so on, creating a puzzle reading that I thought might simply be amusing. When I began reading, my thesis was this: the *Fili* is a mirror text of the *Noli* and was written clearly to revise the first. His first novel is only a palimpsest; his second novel is the text. But what I found, oddly enough, was also the converse: read in tandem with the *Fili*, the *Noli* gains complexity and texture as a strangely doubled text, as if the rich and fluent *Fili* also lives in it, a ghost within its machine.

In the end, these mirror texts told me a story of Rizal as a novelist and of other ways to think about nation.

My rereading project really was to recover Rizal as an artist. True, that was also my goal in writing my second novel, *The Revolution According to Raymundo Mata*. But in that case, I did not just read—I double-crossed Rizal and wrote an entirely new novel, co-opting him. And I've always wondered why in that novel I never had Raymundo Mata actually read the *Fili*— my favorite Rizal text. As I wrote *Raymundo Mata*, I kept deferring Raymundo Mata's reading of the *Fili*—and in the end, he never does get to read the book. And I still wonder why. (Yes, even I wonder about my weird novels.)

What might come from this project of rereading Rizal is a portrait of a writer questioning his means, I thought, wondering through his second novel about his first novel's choices. I've been told there is yet no book on Rizal as a novelist, which does not surprise me. Rizal's use of perspective, or narration modes, for instance, rarely comes up in discussions of Rizaliana, though some cultural thesis on sampaguitas, opium addiction, or student life in Manila could be well served by a close reading of the books' choices of discourse. (Note: the flower sampaguita comes up only once in the *Fili*, a novel mostly set in Manila, but seven times in the *Noli*—thrice in proximity to María Clara, in mixes of omniscient third and free indirect discourse; once in relation to the dead—in a cemetery where Ibarra looks for his father's absent corpse; and the rest in provincial ceremonies, both secular and religious, in direct discourse, or what I call the pueblo, or mass, voice in Rizal: the *sampaga* in the rural *Noli* is related to Rizal's nation imagery; its symbolism disappears in the urban *Fili*.)

I'm not exactly sure when I decided that the *Noli* is the less interesting text. It may have been my own teenage aversion to bad romance. I was in high school when I first read the *Noli*, in Tagalog, and I was very disappointed in Maria Clara, the romantic object whose life ends up not so good. It's through the pathos of Maria Clara that murderous wrath against the Spanish friars has the most righteous cause in Rizal's novels.

My trite formulation has been that the *Noli* is great as propaganda but not as artful as the *Fili*.

When I was reading Rizal for *The Revolution According to Raymundo Mata*, I began to think that the nation's sensibilities are still tied to his favored nineteenth-century romances: the pop melodrama of Victor Hugo and Alexandre Dumas that so enthralled Jose Rizal. If the Filipino novel is germinated by Rizal, then Rizal's tastes tell me nineteenth-century French blockbusters, like Eugene Sue's *Mysteries of Paris* and Hugo's *Les Misérables*, have been ironed into our DNA. And the *Noli*'s voice, to me, seems more tuned to the Frenchmen Hugo, Sue, and Dumas than to their younger, seemingly more experimental contemporary, Flaubert. I kept wishing the *Noli* would read more waywardly, like Machado de Assis's *Philosopher or Dog?* or *Dom Casmurro*. As I read his letters and miscellanea, I kept looking for signs that Rizal had even read Flaubert. I knew he traveled Europe with the work of seventeenth-century Tagalog poet Francisco Balagtas. Balagtas's romantic spirit runs through the *Noli*, along with candid Voltairean hijinks wit. One can imagine Rizal doing selfies with *Florante at Laura* as prop in some coffee shop in Heidelberg. These assured tones— anticlerical humor and romantic agon, Voltaire and Balagtas both—combine in the *Noli*'s editorializing, omniscient narration.

Benedict Anderson, in *Under Three Flags*, notes that Rizal had one book by Flaubert in his library and many by Dumas. I know from Rizal's letters that he loved Eugene Sue, *The Wandering Jew* in particular, now a fairly unreadable novel (at least to me; I tried and found it ghastly), but I wished to know whether he was familiar with that exemplar of style indirect libre, or free indirect discourse—Flaubert—since after all he did write the *Noli* while traveling mostly to and from Paris. I had this theory that my enjoyment of the *Fili* has to do with the fluidity of Rizal's narration modes in the book—an entertaining, complex, para-Flaubertian style. (I recognize that this happens to turn on my own taste in novel-making. I accept that my comments are shot through by my own views of art. I also accept that my concerns with Rizal's texts are technical. I read books, from Gayl Jones to *Tom Jones*, for instruction on my own writing.)

But I did not need to find Flaubert under Rizal's pillow to confirm my idea about narration modes; I just needed to read the *Noli* and the *Fili* in tandem, one chapter after another, and compare them.

Free indirect discourse is a supple narration that enters multiple consciousnesses within an omniscient frame. The psychological acuities of Henry James and the comic shrewdness of Jane Austen (to mention just two novelists who have taught me a lot) arise from those authors' fabulous control of this third-person form. Free indirect discourse allows for multiple and contingent authorities and, in turn, also plays tricks with the reader's consciousness. The nineteenth-century novels of Dumas and Hugo, beloved of Rizal, enthralling in other ways, indulge mostly in the straight omniscient voice. And it's true that, in general, Rizal does use straight omniscience in both novels; his default mode is a single, ironic voice of authority that delivers his themes with excellent and subtle wit. He's good at it. He follows a good writing workshop mantra: he sticks to his strengths.

Especially in the *Noli*, his godlike, omniscient perch above the fray is a powerful tool to impel reader response—specifically, outrage. Rereading Father Damaso's evil malice at the beginning of the *Noli*, I still get angry. I hate Father Damaso as much as I hated him when I was a kid, and I want to kick him in his stupid, ancient-Roman coño face. For Filipinos, Rizal's *Noli* begets a powerful reader response. It became clear, on rereading, how Rizal's omniscient narration in the *Noli* binds the reader to his seductive bias.

It is important to note that Rizal's omniscient irony is the vessel of speech for the angry Filipino in the text—whom, in fact, Rizal does not picture in chapters 1 and 2 of the *Noli*. Instead, he foregrounds the acts and dialogue of the elites, most of them peninsular Spaniards. In the *Noli*'s opening scenes, Rizal's omniscient voice is therefore the sole witness for the otherwise mute, absent, and angry Filipino. It's a strategic, powerful partnership: his omniscience and our absence whet anti-Spanish rage. And its result, this sharpening of our knives, that is, our reader response, is a prominent part of his novel.

Similarly, in the *Fili*, he begins with the "upper deck," the elite, but it's parallel with the "lower deck," where Filipinos have voices. Reader and narrator are entwined in both novels. We, the reader, are part of Rizal's narrative moves, and shrewd as he was, his choices of narration inevitably bound us to him. Of course, historically, they inspired revolt.

He clearly had a thesis of nation in mind, and he moved his readers in this novel of propaganda that, as we know, worked only too well—it killed him (a narrative consequence I do not recommend). But especially in the *Noli*, his keen sense of readership is crucial and central to its power. Neglecting the role of the reader in the *Noli* diminishes our understanding of the text.

What I found in my rereading was that the fascinating mirroring of the two novels—eerie incidences of twinning in the *Noli* and the *Fili*—further complicated any superficial reading I had of the *Noli*. One of the more obvious mirrorings is the twinning of scenes. The most powerful among these mirrored chapters, for instance, are the parallel chapters 24. *Fili* chapter 24 is titled "Un cadaver." Multiple deaths or decays are imagined in this chapter, but the corpse in question lies in the news Basilio delivers to Simoun, who is on the brink of his revolution plot—the news that Maria Clara is dead.

And what is the parallel chapter in *Noli* chapter 24? Hauntingly, it is the memorable scene of the picnic, when the young lovers are completely blissful and Elias the pilot saves them from the crocodile, and we hear a full poem by Rizal sung in Maria Clara's voice—sweet are the hours in one's native land.

How eerie to have these two chapters 24 side by side, like inverted envelopes in which one scene enfolds the other, so that the news of Maria Clara's death encloses her voice in the past, singing Rizal's distant poem of his country, and the song of Maria Clara in the *Noli* encloses her future as *un cadaver*, destroyed by a priest's lust, in the *Fili*. This twinned incidence, coincidence or not, is chilling and moving. It is correct that the most moving twin chapters of the two books are of Maria Clara—she is the ghost of the dyadic, of the primal memory of wholeness, that haunts Rizal's twin books (and who knows, perhaps Rizal—and so his nation), heightening the social fractures and tragic personal fissions in his texts.

Regarding the dyadic in Maria Clara, that is, her figuration as the site of her beau Crisostomo Ibarra's Freudian primal attachment, I base this on the balikbayan azotea scene in the *Noli* when the two lovers tease each other about how they remembered/did not remember the other during Ibarra's absence. Ibarra's romantic memory of Maria Clara is framed by his recall of Europe: a cosmopolitan, continental, and, according to the narrator, *mentiroso* (lying) effusion that describes Germany, Italy, and Andalusia as much as it recalls Maria Clara.

Maria Clara's sweet, intimate memory is of the past; it encompasses mothers. Her recall is of his mother's death when they were children and the leaves of sage she gave him at her dying, remembering how that day they were united in a shared grief: the loss of a mother. Maria Clara also reminds him (via a fatal love letter she keeps in her bosom) of his father's last words. In that scene, Maria Clara literally binds him to *patria*: patrimony and nation.

Other accidents of analogy occurred as I reread. In chapter 5 of both novels, for instance—in *Fili* chapter 5, Basilio, an orphan, returns home to San Diego on Christmas break; in *Noli* chapter 5, Ibarra, who has just been told why he is now an orphan, is spending his first night home on his return to Manila. Orphan versus orphan return home in these parallel chapters. These hallucinatory mirrorings kept happening as I reread Rizal's two books: funhouse returns of doubling scenes. Of course, it is also my own mind that I see; perhaps hallucination, this diplopia, is my modus operandi. But this rereading in tandem is a productive hallucination I'd recommend—for one thing, this reading in tandem is neither homicidal nor heinous. It is only Borgesian—not murderous, but Menardian.

In the analogy created by this reading in tandem, Ibarra, the upper-class victim of priests, is translated in the *Fili* into Basilio, the lower-class victim of priests. Thus, in the *Fili*, Rizal recasts his hero, turning the upper class into the lower class, and so in the *Noli*, vice versa. And just as after the *Noli*, Simoun transfuses/translates (in Tagalog: nagsalin) into Elias, into what will Basilio, still alive at the end of the *Fili*, transform?

Remember that Rizal was a sculptor, too, familiar with recasting: remolding and overlaying forms.

This sculptural, structural twinning gets underlined in the mirrored narration strategies of chapter 6 of both novels: *Fili* chapter 6 is a flashback, telling the backstory of Basilio, that is, the saga of the education of a poor servant kid. But interestingly, *Noli* chapter 6 is also a flashback, telling the backstory of Capitan Tiago, that is, the saga of how a vacuous wealthy kid becomes wealthier. Constantly, *Noli*'s chapters on the elite become implicated in the saga of the lower classes through analogous mirrorings in the *Fili*. Talk about *demonio de las comparaciones*.

ASYMMETRIES, MIRRORS, AND THE ART OF THE NOVEL

There are, of course, asymmetries that deny my mirroring fancy: Maria Clara's locket (*Noli* chapter 27) returns in the *Fili* in chapters with no numerical hauntings (chapters 4, 8, and 10); many minor characters like the *Noli*'s great Hamletian gravedigger, who has no name, or the *Fili*'s Mautang, who weirdly does, occur only once, though Mautang's sidekick, called *el Carolino* (the Caroline), it turns out, is Juli's brother Tano, one more lost boy from the *Noli*. Not only minor, but some key figures do not recur or double, most significantly the unfound body of the sad, vanished sacristan and haunting child laborer, Crispin. (*Question*: if Tano appears, can Crispin be far behind?) Padre Florentino is a key character, the lone good priest, "an indio cleric," who occurs only in the *Fili*.

But there are enough doublings or returns from *Noli* to *Fili* to fill a baklad or tampipi. Surely one can also say he's just a writer with a narrow imagination—maybe Rizal just doesn't have too many plots. But it is fascinating to imagine how these doublings and analogies in the two novels allow us to imagine Rizal's problems as a writer and his self-critiques. Rizal, in his ephemera, his letters, or his science jottings, is garrulous—about boxing, books, or bagoong. But he never talks much about his art; he talks about problems with nation, not narration.

The amazingly persistent mirroring of structures, characters, scenes, and tropes in the *Noli* and *Fili* tells us that, in some way, the *Fili* does perhaps rewrite the *Noli*. But Rizal does it not, as I had imagined, only by his narration modes but also by his weird doublings. The doublings capture, but in elusive and not strictly absolute ways, how Rizal commented, through the *Fili*, on the *Noli*'s devices. He questioned them, resculpted them, reframed binaries of elites and masses, or indio and Spaniard, or civil and religious, or slave and revolutionary, and so wondered about his art. Someone else can write a whole book on that.

It is only by chapter 7 of the *Noli* that Rizal moves into extended free indirect discourse, in the third-person limited voice of Maria Clara. Most of the novel is in persuasive third-person omniscient, but a fluid omniscience that sometimes veers into an intimate, gossiping plural first. The first trace of extended free indirect discourse in the *Fili* is also the psychological perspective of a woman: Basilio's superstitious girlfriend, Juli. But unlike the *Noli*, by chapter 4 onward, the *Fili* moves easily into multiple third person perspectives, indirect and free indirect modes of various characters—he ventriloquizes the psychological perceptions of the untutored Juli, the unlettered wit of the coachman carrying the medical student Basilio back home, the grief and terror of Basilio confronting the frighteningly radical Simoun in that creepy place of textual doubling, "Ibarra's wood" (which is the site of Elias's death in the *Noli* and entombs both the focus of Basilio's grief, his maddened mother Sisa, and the focus of Simoun's grief, Ibarra's noble friend Elias: not to mention the Gothic death-plot of the land-grabbing colonizer, Ibarra's ancestor with no name), and so on.

So fluid in his use of perspective in the *Fili*, Rizal thus seems to have liberated himself from the straitjacket of the omniscient editorial voice in the *Noli*, giving consciousness to multiple voices in his new, confident, but experimental style, from chapter 4 onward. For such a young writer, working only on his second book, Rizal displays no nerves, making unexpected moves, some noted by Ben Anderson already in readings of the chapter "Tatakut" in *Why Counting Counts*, among his other comments on the *Fili*. It is no wonder the *Fili* is less taught in Philippine high school classes—the book is interested also in consciousness, not just country. Rizal shifts in and out of the minds of casual cynic Pecson, cowardly bully Juanito, opportunistic but oppressed Quiroga—a whole panoply of tipos Manilenses, as Rizal the scientist-cataloger called them—in ways that, for me, seem to acknowledge the flat urgencies of the *Noli*'s singular propaganda voice. But interestingly, even as he moves into fresh narrative territory while recycling old plots, he honors the problems of Filipino discourse he had solved in the *Noli*. A novel quite clearly about the "social cancer" of colonialism, the *Fili* also ponders the art of the novel—pondering, in my view, Rizal's first novel, the *Noli*, in particular.

Chapter 7 is a touchstone passage in both the *Fili's* themes and the *Fili's* art. Chapter 7 of the *Fili* is a gorgeous set piece. Amazingly reflexive, it weaves perhaps one of the most complex reader-writer-text-(language)-nation webs in Philippine writing—that imagined community in novels that I find most persistently engrossing and problematic in my own experience of writing novels. It's important to recognize here that the central plot of the *Fili* puts the novel in reflexive, refractive, mirroring territory. The *Fili's* plot is the reading/writing theme of language itself—a key topic for any writer but, in many ways, the cri de coeur of the Filipino.

The students in chapter 2 are agitating for a Castilian Academy in Manila, a school for teaching Spanish.

Thus, a crisis of language is the plot's pivot.

Rizal asks: Is it revolutionary for Filipinos to learn Spanish?

WHAT'S LANGUAGE GOT TO DO WITH IT?

For me, a novelist, what I hear loudly here is the self-critical question of the writer Rizal: what does it mean for him to be writing a Filipino novel, "hold[ing] a mirror up to nature," in Spanish?

This question implicates the text within this text, the *Noli*—because by the time he was writing the *Fili*, IRL the *Noli*, as we know, had the odd effect of being a bomb, *una mecha*, set among friars who wished to kill him. It was also the fuse, *una mecha*, a call to action, among Filipinos who wished to follow him, precisely for his art-crime of convincingly mirroring (considering any number of projections and misrecognitions such mirroring entails) the conditions of Rizal's Philippines.

In *Fili* chapter 7, Simoun says to Basilio, whom he accuses as a lower-order thinker, that is, a reformist, who does not understand that a Filipino's misplaced faith in Spain's civil authority is a radical failure of self-analysis:

> Go ahead, ask for Hispanization and do not blanch from shame when they tell you no...You want to add another language to the forty-odd we already speak here so we can understand one another even less?

Simoun's continuing speech is a beautiful expletive that explodes, in a singular tongue, the problem of having multiple tongues. He delivers his illuminating rant on the Castilian in illuminating Castilian:

> El español nunca será lenguaje general en el pais, el pueblo nunca lo hablará porque para las concepciones de su cerebro y los sentimientos de su corazon no tiene frases ese idioma: cada pueblo tiene el suyo, como tiene su manera de sentir. ¿Qué vais á conseguir con el castellano, los pocos que lo habeis de hablar?

¡Matar vuestra originalidad, subordinar vuestros pensamientos á otros cerebros y en vez de haceros libres haceros verdaderamente esclavos!

How odd for Simoun to ventriloquize this point that Rizal has, in fact, already made quite moot through the persuasive explosion that was his last novel, the *Noli*:

> Spanish will never be the language of the country, the people of the country will never speak it because for the thoughts of their own mind and sentiments of their heart that idiom does not have phrases: each people has its own tongue, as it has its own manner of feeling. What will you gain with Spanish, the few who will speak it? Kill your originality, subordinate your thoughts to others' minds and instead of gaining your freedom make yourselves truly into slaves!

> (all translations are from the Penguin Classic editions of *Noli Me Tangere* and *El Filibusterismo*, translated by Harold Augenbraum)

The breathtaking reflexivity in this passage is contradictory, provocative, and dizzying on several levels. One, Simoun, speaking in Spanish, convicts himself as one of the *verdaderamente esclavos* (truly enslaved); two, Basilio, understanding Simoun's Spanish (he functions, too, as the reader's proxy in the passage), is thus complicit and so also *esclavo*; three, the Filipino reader who understands Simoun's Spanish is also part of the textual crime, that is, *esclavo*; four, the novel, written in Spanish, is destabilized explicitly by the writer who devised this passage denouncing *el español* in *español*; and five, the writer, writing in Spanish, convicts himself, too, by the damning words he fashions in Simoun's oracular voice. (Only the Filipino who does not read, write, or speak Spanish is null in this speech—a question for a different essay.)

This conviction by language—to play on that English pun—raises the specter (or speculum, Latin for mirror, as Rizal's pedant Sybila might note, using one more of Rizal's tongues) of that great mirror-novel hidden in the *Fili*—that is, the *Noli*. But he (and we) also know the *Noli* has paradoxically already opened the eyes of the *verdaderamente esclavos*—in some sense freeing them (and in terms of the *Noli*'s reach, this is true not only of those Filipinos who read Spanish but also extends its voice to us, those who read it in translation, in its wake).

And so Rizal questions both the *Noli* and himself, wondering about his own originality and subordination, one of "the few who will speak it." At the same time, he frees himself from the bondage of being the iconic author of the *Noli*, indicted by Simoun as a suspect text, while also, oddly enough, recognizing the *Noli*'s power.

By what awry, magical stroke, then, does Rizal in this passage complicate his novels but also conjure the problems of the Filipino reader of his novels?

He creates a destabilized, reflexive people who must cross-examine who they are. Or, in a sense, they must recognize themselves through misrecognition as a constantly lost and yet also found figure of translation—translation being the site of their lost-and-profound humanity—when they read the nation in Rizal's words.

This is the crux of ourselves as a nation—and the problem of all our novelists. We exist indelibly in translation, even among ourselves as fellow speakers of our intramural Filipino languages—Ilonggo or Waray or Tagalog or Ilocano or Cebuano and so on—but also in relation to our power speeches (currently English, though Tagalog is also a "colonizer" language in some spaces). We are subjected, and mediated, and lost yet found in our multiple texts—and tongues. We are thus born, in Simoun's speech, into the reality of our multiple speech selves.

Very early on, like a prescient prophet of our "postcoloniality," as some call our traumatic yet also utterly human condition, Rizal in his novels grapples explicitly with the labyrinth of language that defines us.

As the student Sandoval exclaims in *Fili* chapter 14: "What does the integrity of the state have to do with the rules of syntax?!"

Well, Rizal, the reflexive novelist, might say—*everything*.

THE ART OF THE SPHINX

Of course, one must also take Simoun's speech with a grain of salt. Rizal's dialogues are diabolically dialectical. To be honest, as a writer, I most envy Rizal's skill as a pellucid debater of plural ideas in conversations, powerful in both the *Noli* and the *Fili*. It's hard to do because you must imagine conviction on both sides; they each must have their own humanity and stakes.

Rizal's correct choice is to do it in formula, as a pattern, a recurring weave that the reader expects. In *Fili* chapter 7, one is meant to refract Simoun's speech through Basilio's (the proxy reader's) modest skepticism in the scene. As the novel unfolds, Simoun—versus such idealists as the poet Isagani or hopeful cynics like the student Pecson and so on—keeps shape-shifting: he is a masked, unstable truth-teller.

This ambiguity is deliberate. Rizal is very aware of personalities as analogies, *comparaciones* rather than singularities, existing within a dialectic of ideas and forces, not simply as a flat image without a glass backing—without a mirror of comparisons. It is hard to see the elite Simoun without seeing his translation, or reflection, in the poor orphan Basilio in the scenes they have with each other, or to view the poet Isagani without his twin, lawyer Señor Pasta, or his other co-duelist, Father Fernandez. Enfolded in Isagani are the demands of law and church. Scene by scene, Rizal keeps projecting one character in the other, and not only that, one book into the other, mirroring perhaps the multiplicity of his own desires and, more obviously, the rigors of his highly reflexive intellect.

It's hard to be a hero if your mind can consistently hold two contradictory notions at once.

But in many ways, that is a novelist's job.

As I noted in the novel *Raymundo Mata*, it is no accident that in Rizal's two books, the middle name—or matronymic—of Ibarra, his hero, is Magsalin, an infinitive verb, a pun, meaning both to translate and to transfuse blood. To me, the name shows how aware Rizal was of words, homonyms, and doubling texts running in our veins. In his *Miscellaneous Writings*, a notebook jotting his daily observations as a student, he gossips about his friends, such as the risk-taking fop, Pedro Paterno, in code—even IRL Rizal's a word trickster.

In the Quiapo Fair chapter of the *Fili*, called "Supercherías," or Tricks, the character Simoun, who is really Ibarra in disguise, gets a magician to set up a talking Sphinx's head to entertain a group of priests, who include Padre Salvi, María Clara's abuser. The Sphinx's head tells an ancient Egyptian story about a powerful priest's lust for a defenseless girl. The reader understands that the *supercheria*, or trick, is that through the magician's hidden mirrors, it is Simoun, as Sphinx, who is fabricating this tale that mirrors details of Padre Salvi's abuse. Padre Salvi faints as he hears his secrets told aloud in the dark magician's den.

One hears Rizal laughing as he sets up the unexpected cryptogram for resurrecting that cryptic head in the *Fili*'s Quiapo Fair chapter. The password, the code for the Sphinx's speech, is *Deremof*. Deremof is an anagram, not in his novel's Spanish but in unexpected yet prophetic English. (By the way, Rizal makes zero effort to help us figure this out.) The oracular code *Deremof* is this instructive and amazing, double-tongued sword. *Deremof* is the anagram of the nation's desire, but Rizal in the Spanish-language novel *Fili* speaks that desire in scrambled English.

Deremof = freedom.

Researching the Philippine-American war, when I recall this prolepsis—this linguistic future-telling in the *Fili*, by which Rizal oddly leaps toward the nation's capture, two years after his death, by America—my head spins.

Any consideration of the representation of the elite or of peasants, or of the diaspora, or of womanhood and any other similar themes must consider the profoundly analogical, refractive acts of representation that run through these novels. I do not see anything flat in the work of Rizal. There is trickery in his texts. I read him as a demonic comparative thinker—highly aware of readership, or acts of reading and writing in the text.

For instance, I note Rizal's name for the Sphinx-head in "Supercherías"—its name is Imuthis—so I scrambled it for other, possible anagrams: Himuti (s) in Tagalog would be someone becoming pale or white. But one more scrambling came up with *himitsu*. It's a Japanese word—and it's significant here that Rizal had spent some months in Japan, with an alleged Japanese sweetheart to boot. In addition, japonaiserie was all the rage in Paris at the time: in one of his letters, Rizal notes how at a museum he is mistaken for Japanese, and just for fun, he pretend-speaks Japanese to the white man, enacting one more innocent anticolonial subversion.

The word *himitsu*, in Japanese, means secret.

If we give credit to discretion in Rizal's Sphinx-like, riddling art practice, even this secret he declined to reveal. Again, nothing in extensive, published Rizaliana has mentioned this code.

Rizal was a trickster; he liked secrets, jokes, puns.

These art gestures in his novels must be front and center in any reading of his words—and thus of ourselves. Even in his practice as a novelist, he exercised a grounding political ethos—reflexivity. He found a way to reread himself, and so forged his fresh, astonishing style in the *Fili*. He creates, in the figure of Simoun, his unsparing twin of himself, a doppelganger—a desperate, despairing fixer of plots.

That is, a fictionist.

WHERE THE BALL NOT YET IS

Too often, we fail to imagine Rizal as a writer who is creating fiction, though yes, a persistent reading of nation, Rizal's Philippines, conjured in the fascinatingly unstable mirror of his words, dominates the text.

We often think of the *Fili*'s ending—that disappointing, vacillating response to revolution in the scene of Simoun's death—as Rizal's absolute commentary on revolution. But it's also possible to see Rizal as more Gramscian than not: the concept of "decisive conjuncture" might be a good way to think about revolution and Rizal. The founder of Italy's Communist Party, Antonio Gramsci, emphasizes how revolution (but sadly also devolution) is a contingent matter, the success of which depends on the ability to analyze correctly and seize the historical moment. The *Fili* is a novel always in the contingent moment of revolution—its outcome is contingent even as it ends. Its decisive moment is still in suspense.

On the other hand, it's odd how Rizal failed in his work to fully envision contemporary, real-life revolutionary figures like Mabini or Bonifacio, *verdaderos filibusteros* par excellence, who seem to exist on a different historical plane than the novels, though Mabini and Bonifacio both avidly read Rizal.

I like to think that Rizal, like any other novelist, imagined himself writing his next book. A writer, like a good soccer player, plays toward that spot in the future—where the ball not yet is. The Victorian novel, as we know, was historically read in threes, called triple-deckers. I like to imagine Rizal had that third book in mind.

But as we also know, Rizal did not live to write, or finish, another novel. In this sense, what happens after the *Fili* is still undone, unwritten, perhaps like the nation or revolution?

But the ending of the *Fili* can also be seen as Rizal's artistic response to the *Noli*. What psychological acuities, aesthetic considerations, and political moves are gained, refashioned, and lost when one moves into unfixed and vagabond free indirect discourse? You have a more reflective, doubting, politically and psychologically ambiguous character in Simoun—more ambiguous certainly than the mourned-for, faithful Elias—because, like any emerging writer (he was not yet thirty after all, still okay for the Whiting Award), Rizal's narrative technique had changed.

I imagine this as his conundrum: what to think of his very effective *Noli* as he enjoys a different way to write? Can a writer molt from his first book, leaving it behind? His was not quite the dilemma of the second-book author, but let's imagine. As if it were the nation's treasured, precious *Noli* that at the end of the *Fili* the priest Florentino throws into the sea, his encomium on the *Noli* being this invocation, which ends *El Filibusterismo*: "When men need you for a holy, sublime reason, God will pull you from the bosom of your waves."

Few Filipinos would wish to withhold from the *Noli* those adjectives— holy and sublime. Not I.

On one level, as noted, the *Fili* is a university novel, and many of its powerful scenes in free indirect discourse are set among students. I've written three university novels about revolt, and so I do see my biases here—in fact, my book *Gun Dealers' Daughter* was written with the *Fili* in mind, including a character whose rebel name is Simoun.

Among Rizal's student chapters, my favorite is chapter 13 in the *Fili*, "La clase de fisica." After considering the dizzying puzzle of mirror structures in Rizal's two novels, how fascinating to read that this chapter centers on the trope that illuminates what I consider Rizal's major device for evoking the nation in his novel diptych, as literary theorist Neil Garcia names the pair of novels, the *Noli* and the *Fili*, so uniting them as one.

(Though, as I said, for me, I see Rizal going for the triple-decker. One of my speculations that I sent Anderson: if the rediscovered, unfinished *Makamisa*, found by historian Ambeth Ocampo in mislabeled folders in the National Archives, were the third novel, begun in Tagalog, with a character named Ysagani, a religious kid luckless in love, *Makamisa* could hint at a flashback history, going back further in time, in analepsis, way before the *Noli*. Rizal's use of the name Ysagani I link to the good priest Florentino, whose backstory is also about lost love. Padre Florentino is the figure who throws Simoun's jewel box into the ocean at the end of the *Fili*. Why is he the book's last character? Because his story jumpstarts the next one. I'd make Padre Florentino's first name be Ysagani; thus, Ysagani Florentino, who later has a nephew who bears his name. Basilio, the doctor-orphan, and Isagani, the priest's nephew, happen to be the last rebel students standing in the *Fili*—thus, in the third novel, Basilio and Isagani would herald the new Filipino. So I told Ben Anderson. I knew Ben loved speculation; he took my bait, and he wrote me back. Unfortunately, he died before we finished the conversation. His last words to me were: "You make it very interesting!!!!"—four exclamation points. And now I will never know just how crazy he thought my idea was.)

In *Fili* chapter 13, a satirical chapter set in a physics class, Rizal's illuminating plot device is a mirror. Padre Millon, the sadistic physics teacher who is also an idiot, makes students memorize a numbing definition of that basic subject of materials physics: *un espejo*—

> Se da el nombre de espejo á toda superficie pulimentada, destinada á producir por la reflexion de la luz las imágenes de los objetos situados delante de dicha superficie por las sustancias que forman estas superficies se dividen en espejos metálicos y espejos de cristal...

> The name mirror is given to all polished surfaces, destined to produce by the reflection of light the images of objects placed in front of said surface by substances that form these surfaces divided into metallic mirrors and glass mirrors...

This theme of reflexivity, or reflection, or doubling, or mirroring, becomes the literal center of this chapter satirizing education in Spanish in the Philippines (and is succeeded by the Quiapo Fair chapter on mirror tricks, and so on), thus causing a vertigo of refraction in this self-referential text. Because the novel, of course—any novel, really—but especially this novel, is also a trick with mirrors, as is Imuthis/Ibarra's storytelling deception in the Quiapo chapter: "Destined to produce by the reflection of light the images of objects placed in front of said surfaces..."

This scene of the mirror in a physics class conjures another vertigo of images—an infinite regression of reflections that is the fatal, unstable condition of novel-writing, a knowing deception that attempts truth, but also a "truth" founded on "tricks" (*supercherías*)—enclosing as a novel does the projections and mirrorings of the reader, the writer, the novel, and the world it hopes to mirror (which includes the reader, the writer, and so on, ad infinitum). When we address the *Fili* by a close reading of his narration moves, Rizal's work becomes a text somewhat like Borges's Library of Babel, a vertiginous mirror of a universe—in Rizal's case, more modestly, a nation. "Whimsical," yes, but intriguing.

THAT FLEETING ACT

By trying to describe what the novels were doing as novels, I found myself in a surprising conversation with Rizal's books. I experienced a pleasure that I had not realized before I sat down to describe their effects. By closely reading the novels for their art moves, instead of depending on my own hazy memories of my prejudices, I learned to appreciate the *Noli* in ways that had escaped me, and my rereading taught me to imagine a writer's secret moves that, too, had eluded me.

In Raymundo Mata's pursuit of Rizal in my book *The Revolution According to Raymundo Mata*, Raymundo's deep disappointment in Dapitan was that he never saw signs of Rizal writing. It is as if, ultimately, by this gap, Raymundo could not be with Rizal—in intimacy, in knowing. And now perhaps I can tentatively answer why, in that novel, my character Raymundo kept trying but never read the *Fili*—I could never actually picture Rizal revising, which, to me, is the heart of writing. I could not see him so vulnerable.

Reading his novels in tandem for this project, I finally pictured him in that fleeting, painfully mortal, ordinary act, central to my own concept of writing and too often absent in our concept of Rizal, or perhaps more dangerously, our concept of nation: the act of revision.

Rereading the *Fili* and *Noli* in tandem, I finally found Rizal revising. And in this sense, through doubling, I finally found my elusive intimacy—as a novelist, as a reader, as a Filipino—with Rizal. It is my own private Rizal, of course. But after all, it is this dyadic communing, this impossible striving for intimacy, if not wholeness, that all of us want, and which language tells us we will not consummate. And yet, we try.

VERNADETTE VICUÑA GONZALEZ

Our Loving Hula Hands, or Lessons from a Sometime Student

My first encounter with hula was as a child in the Philippines. I still have a photograph of that moment.

I was three years old and enrolled in a free community preschool program in my birthplace, Dumaguete City. I was onstage, dressed in a ruffled bikini top and a red artificial grass skirt, with flowers around one wrist. I was still wearing my white ankle socks—unlike the rest of my classmates who were barefoot—an overlooked detail that irked my mother. One of my classmates was holding artificial grass pompoms.

We were performing a dance to "Pearly Shells." To this day, I remember some of the hand motions from the choreography. Hawai'i was not a concept any of us understood, even as we found ourselves dancing to its music. For a decade or two after Hawai'i's statehood in 1959, all things Hawai'i were the rage in the Philippines. Fueled by the rise of mass tourism, following the routes of military planes and ships that traversed the Pacific bases of the United States and packed in balikbayan boxes of migrant Filipinos, hula made its way to me in the mid-1970s, well before I made my way to Hawai'i decades later as a professor at the university.

Later on, when I was already teaching at the University of Hawai'i, I learned about Don Ho, the most famous of several singers who recorded a version of "Pearly Shells" in 1965 and probably the reason why the song became a hit in the Philippines.[1] Later still, I discovered that Nora Aunor, that mainstay of Philippine entertainment, had recorded "Pearly Shells" in 1971 as part of *Blue Hawaii*, her album of Hawai'i-themed songs.[2] The title of her album was a riff on Elvis's film musical of the same name from a decade earlier.

Aunor's single sold over a million copies, which is likely why I found myself at three, in socks and an artificial grass skirt, miming lyrics about shells covering the shore. On her album, there was only one song originally written in Hawaiian, Queen Lili'uokalani's "Aloha 'Oe."[3] Aunor sang the English version, minus the title phrase, which remained in Hawaiian.[4] The rest of the songs on her album were standards of the burgeoning tourist entertainment circuit, from "Tiny Bubbles" and "My Little Grass Shack" to "Little Brown Gal."

Despite having a Filipina rendition of "Pearly Shells," it was Don Ho's version we danced to in the Philippines. Perhaps Don Ho's version carried the fantasy of Hawai'i with more authority than Nora Aunor's: American tropics often became substitutes for each other. Don Ho was *the* entertainer whose shows in Waikīkī the tiki bar tourists flocked to. He appeared on television shows and even got his own televised variety show, right when mass tourism exploded in Hawai'i. And perhaps it would have been too much for young girls to be dancing to the racier lyrics of "Little Brown Gal," regardless of whose version it was: *I'll be leaving soon but the thrill I enjoy/Is not the island moon nor the fish and the poi/It's just a little brown gal in a little grass skirt/In a little grass shack in Hawai'i.*[5] It would not have been so far off from another tune, "My Filipino Baby," which became popular during the Philippine-American War.[6] (That song poked fun of Black soldiers becoming enamored with dark-skinned Filipinas. In later versions, sung by white men, references to race faded away, but racialized desire remained.) "Pearly Shells" was the most G-rated version of these acquisitive fantasies.

Long after my lone preschool dance performance, my mother hums "Pearly Shells." It is part of the soundtrack of my childhood. It is a catchy melody with easy-to-learn choreography. I can see why it became a fad at the time.

It was not until graduate school, when I started studying Hawai'i and the Philippines as two places indelibly marked and linked by U.S. imperialism, that I learned that "Pearly Shells" overlays English lyrics on the melody of an old Hawaiian language song called "Pupu a 'o 'Ewa" (Shells of 'Ewa).[7]

The song's Hawaiian lyrics are not about "pearly shells/from the ocean/ shining in the sun, covering the shore" but instead reference the discovery of pearl oysters at Pu'uloa, the Hawaiian name for what is today called Pearl Harbor.

The song cites the abundance of sustenance in the waters of Pu'uloa, which historically encompassed an impressive array of fishponds and taro patches fed by estuaries, aquifers, and fresh water springs. Pu'uloa was also the home of Ka'ahupāhau, the shark deity who, until appeased, infamously sabotaged early attempts to construct the first U.S. Navy dry dock in 1913.[8]

Now the lagoon houses an active U.S. military base and, designated as a Superfund site, is a dumping ground for fuel and other petroleum products stored underground, fuel that has been leaking into the aquifer and poisoning people. The U.S. military secured access to the harbor by virtue of a "reciprocity" treaty that followed on the heels of a revised constitution that Hawai'i's king was forced to sign at the point of a bayonet in 1887.

When I see them my heart tells me that I love you/More than all the little pearly shells. The English-language version of "Pearly Shells," which speaks of tropical desire woven into a Hollywood soundtrack and tourism's promise of aloha, does not praise the bounty of the land and waters of Puʻuloa to be shared among its people. It does not describe the shark deity who safeguarded the waters. When I danced to it at three, I was blissfully ignorant of the way the song and steps trampled over a sacred space for Hawaiians.

I don't know why it took me so long to ask to be a student of hula in Honolulu. Maybe it was a lingering embarrassment from my naive first encounter, blissfully unaware of the perils of imperialism.

***

I finally started taking hula lessons as an adult after my oldest child had been dancing for over a decade with their teacher, Kumu Hula Snowbird Bento. For over ten years, every Saturday morning, I accompanied my child to a university classroom at the School of Hawaiian Knowledge. While waiting outside the room where the youngest students took class, I received hula lessons by proxy. I realized the enormity of the gift of a settler Filipinx child being able to learn from their kumu.

Sometimes, there would be no hula lesson, but rather a morning spent cleaning up on the grounds around the classroom—weeding, culling dead ti leaves from their stalks, and hauling trash bags of green waste—lessons of care and reciprocity under the hot sun.

When I finally went to my first class as a student, we learned the hula to "Kulāiwi," a song composed by Larry Kauanoe Kimura.[9] And what Kumu Snowbird meant by *learn* wasn't just about memorizing the words or the technique of the song, but taking in its significance and history—so that when we danced the hula, we embodied its meaning in our movements. Kulāiwi means the land of my ancestors or homeland. Kula signifies a plain or pasture, open country, and iwi means bone, and in Hawaiʻi, the iwi of the dead are cherished, sacred, and hidden.

The song is a reminder to a beloved descendant of Hāloa that they are the children of the land and that this claim to the land is their birthright and cannot be purchased. It is also a reminder that caring for the land is their responsibility and right as a native child and as a Hawaiian. The mele ends with a declaration: I am a Hawaiian for now and forever. He Hawaiʻi au mau a mau.

The hula to "Kulāiwi" is a beautiful love song in motion. We dance a smooth back and forth kāholo to the first strains of the ʻukulele. From "Mai ka piʻina a ka lā i Haʻehaʻe," we trace an arc overhead with one arm, as if describing the path of the sun from its starting point of Haʻehaʻe, the easternmost end of Hawaiʻi. We stretch our arms to either side, gliding them forward until they almost meet in front of us, as if to encompass the geography that ends with the islet of Lehua. The stories of hula are often about land, the rains or breezes that fall upon it, the life sustained by it, and the relations to the ancestors that are animated and remembered through caring for the land and each other. We track the contours of Kulāiwi's geography with our bodies and relay its history with the harmony of our voices.

When I started to take lessons, I learned more intimately how radical the practice of hula is and how it embodies and imparts lessons in history, geography, culture, science, and politics. The first lesson is permission. One cannot even enter the space of the hālau without asking for and being granted permission. I learned the chant asking for permission to enter, so I could chant it confidently with my hula sisters. Mai pa'a i ka leo, he 'ole ka hea mai. When the kumu chants the reply to enter, she uses an expression that invites the student to be fed. Hula is sustenance.[10]

There are two kinds of hula. Hula kahiko, or ancient hula, which I prefer, is accompanied by percussion with chanted tunes, and the movement tends to be more forceful. Kulāiwi is a hula in the 'auana style, which is softer and fluid. Hula 'auana songs are sung, often with beautiful harmonies. It's the style most of the world is familiar with because it developed after Western colonialism. It is the style that Haunani Kay-Trask, another kumu, has described as featuring the "lovely hula hands" that tourists translate as an open invitation.[11]

But in its flowing lyricism, its declaration of kuleana—of responsibility and rights—dancing to "Kulāiwi" turns into a gentle but steadfast assertion of loyalty. My child reminds me that our kumu has taught us that in hula, you tell a story with your hands. The graceful gestures of Kulāiwi remind me that all this beauty is born from a fierce commitment to that land and its people.

As I learned the song and the hula, I wondered if someone like me, a Filipina settler, could rightfully dance to this song. Kumu Snowbird taught me that, while I am not Hawaiian, I am a child of this land that nurtures me, and I, too, have responsibilities to it. This is the hula that is the backbone of my relationship to Hawai'i. He Hawai'i au mau a mau. For me, this is less a claim to Hawaiian identity than a declaration of loyalty and solidarity.

This lesson is one of the reasons I found myself on the mauna twice in 2019.

***

It is the middle of December 2019, and we are gathered at the foot of the mountain. It is noon, and time for the midday protocol to honor the mountain and restate our commitment to its protection. The sun warms our bodies as we stand next to each other on the asphalt road. We are young, old, somewhere in between; Hawaiian, not Hawaiian; all genders; from Big Island, from neighbor islands, from all over the world. Most of us are wearing jackets, hats, and shoes to ward off the chill, but there are some who are barefoot or just wearing a malo. Those who know the hula or who want to learn are invited to dance and chant.

The crisp breeze ripples the flags that line both sides of the road. The mountain is massive; we face its summit in the distance and feel it firm, steady, and vast under our feet. We turn to the kūpuna, some of them sheltered in a large tent who have held their ground for months now. Just beyond them, a barricade made of bamboo blocks the access road to the summit, putting a stop to the construction of the Thirty Meter Telescope.

The hula starts with two beats of the drum. We clap our hands together and begin the chant, "He aha lā he kūkulu?"[12] Our voices blend together with the drumbeat as we ask, *What is a pillar?* Our hips rotate—'ami—and our knees are slightly bent, anchoring our bodies to the earth. When we answer the question—*A mountain!*—we delicately touch the fingers of one hand to the open palm of the other. We repeat the gesture, switching hands and sketching a fleeting miniature of the mountain's gentle slope. Everyone takes two steps forward as we 'ami again: two slow circles, three in a quick spiral, and then two slower, while our hands clap together in rhythm. We inhale the cold air in between verses.

We ask again three more times, *What is a pillar?* We move forward as a body each time to answer—He 'ahu! He pōhaku! He kanaka! Our arms trace the gestures for an altar, a rock, or a person. We start again from the beginning, repeating the chant twice more, each time louder and with more urgency. We get closer to each other, moving like one organism closer to the kūpuna. Our voices blend under the boundless sky. The hula ends abruptly, with a last beat, and we disperse, making way for another part of the protocol on the mountain.

There are other chants, other hula, that are part of the protocol, but this is the one I know best, and it is one that is most forgiving for people just learning it. This is my second pilgrimage to the mountain this year, to the improvised camp that had sprung up at the base of Mauna a Wākea on the Big Island following the arrest of kūpuna and others who refused to give way to the construction machines the previous summer.

I came with two good friends from the university where I work, which also happens to be the university sponsoring the construction of the telescope that many Native Hawaiians have rejected.

We are there with hundreds of people, some who have come to be present for a day or two, like us, and others who have been there for the long haul, sleeping in tents dotting the lava field. Occasionally, a car or van pulls over on the shoulder of the road near the encampment. The drivers drop off blankets, bananas from their gardens, or warm meals for the kūpuna.

I had first come to the mountain in July with a friend, shortly after the kūpuna had been arrested. Even during the summer, it was chilly at night. On that earlier trip, we had brought sleeping bags and coats, gift cards to buy food, and tents to blunt the cold for those who were called to be on the mauna.

It is even colder now in December, and the thousands-strong gathering that I was a part of in July has since thinned out to a few hundred. Still, they hold the road.

The hula hālau I belong to, Ka Pā Hula O Ka Lei Lehua, is among those hula schools whose kumu have taken a clear stance to protect Mauna a Wākea as a site sacred to Native Hawaiians. Our hālau has been learning other hula composed specifically for the mauna, and my kumu has brought other members of the hālau to the mauna in the intervening months. That Ka Pā Hula O Ka Lei Lehua would be among the hālau going to the mauna, or present at the capitol to protest state collusion, or holding community gatherings and teach-ins, was completely in alignment with the principles of aloha ʻāina, or love and care for the land, that are at the heart of hula practice. Hula hālau were among those at the forefront of the gathering at the mauna, because students of hula would find the idea of building a telescope on sacred land to be in conflict with aloha ʻāina.

On the mauna, permission had not been granted. Permission had not even been sought.

***

The mauna isn't the only place where protocol is held. Because the University of Hawaiʻi at Mānoa is the main culprit pushing for the Thirty Meter Telescope to be built, some of its students occupied one of the administrative buildings, demanding that the president resign.

That fall, they start the semester with a sit-in protest. On the manicured lawn in front of the building they have retaken, they erect bamboo structures honoring the thirty-eight kūpuna arrested while blocking the access road to Mauna a Wākea. They hold protocol at the ʻahu daily, at the same times that protocol is held at the mauna. They show up faithfully until the pandemic hit and everything got suspended. Even the kūpuna on the mauna went home while keeping a watchful eye on the mountain. But that fall and into the spring of 2020, the students hold protocol, three times a day, every day. In the few times I am able to join them, I am the student. I follow the undergraduates who have been unwavering. This, too, is a lesson of hula.

On campus, on this day, we are led by a young man whose deep voice carries around the circle we have formed. I take my shoes off so I can feel the grass under my feet. We are a motley group of students, staff, and faculty, and we greet each other, sweating in the day's humidity.

I trip over the words to "Nā ʻAumākua," a petition to ancestors for protection and guidance.[13]

I think about my ancestors, the ones of my lineage, as well as those I have claimed and who have claimed me. I think, too, about the ancestors I'd rather not claim. The Philippines is full of ancestors who were warriors as well as those who were traitors.

I think about how I don't know a single prayer in Bisaya, my mother tongue, but I know some of the words to this one.

Our leader begins the chant to "Oli Kūkulu," another mele about pillars, and I am reminded that to protect the mauna, to protect the lands and waters that feed us all, in the places that we used to call home and in the places we now call home, we will need all of us.[14]

The mele calls on the beloved warriors, guardians, and protectors that make up the "pillars, the four cardinal points," to rise. It calls on the Natives of Hawai'i to rise, on the relatives of the Pacific to rise, and on the relations on Turtle Island to rise. It also calls on the rest of us, as friends and supporters from around the world, to rise alongside them.

Our voices ring out and up, calling and responding to our leader's prompts.

ALOHA 'ĀINA!

KŪKULU!

EŌ!

HŪ!

KŪ!

KŪ'Ē!

ALOHA!

OLA!

HŪ!

We finish protocol, bid each other aloha, and return to work.

ACKNOWLEDGMENTS
Maraming salamat to the generous readers who gave invaluable feedback: Rani Neutill, Mimi Thi Nguyen, Yutian Wong, and Laurel Flores Fantauzzo.

NOTES
1. Don Ho, "Pearly Shells," in *Don Ho's Greatest Hits* (Warner Records, 1966).
2. Nora Aunor, *Blue Hawaii* (Philippines: Alpha Records Corporation, 1971).

3. Lili'uokalani, 1838–1917, "Aloha Oe Farewell to Thee / Words and Music by H.M. Queen Liliuokalani," UHM Library Digital Image Collections, accessed April 10, 2024, https://digital.library.manoa.hawaii.edu/items/show/31961. The description in the catalog of the University of Hawai'i at Mānoa's digital collections is worth quoting at length here: "Written in 1877 or 1878 by Queen Lili'uokalani but transcribed during the period of her 10-month house arrest (1895-1896), 'Aloha Oe,' (Farewell To Thee) can be read as both a love song and a statement of Hawaiian sovereignty. In the years since its composition, it has been adopted, adapted, revised and/or plagiarized for a variety of purposes: Jack London used the title for a short story about a doomed love affair between a mid-western girl and a Hawaiian boy; Elvis Presley sang a version in the film *Blue Hawaii*. Dating from 1908 through 1940, the various editions of 'Aloha Oe' sheet music held by UH-Mänoa's Hamilton Library document America's increasing fascination with the Hawaiian Islands following annexation and leading up to World War II."

4. See also Adria Imada, "'Aloha 'Oe': Settler-Colonial Nostalgia and the Genealogy of a Love Song," ed. Patrick Wolfe, *American Indian Culture and Research Journal* 37, no. 2 (January 2013): 35–52, https://escholarship.org/uc/item/8vb4s2dd.

5. "Little Brown Gal" was composed in 1935 by Don McDiarmid, J. Noble, and Lee Wood, lyrics accessed April 10, 2024, https://www.huapala.org/Li/Little_Brown_Gal.html.

6. Music Division, The New York Public Library, "My Filipino Baby," New York Public Library Digital Collections, accessed April 10, 2024, https://digital collections.nypl.org/items/510d47df-f042-a3d9-e040-e00a18064a99. The song was recorded years later by country music singer Ernest Tubb.

7. "Pūpū A O 'Ewa," lyrics and translation accessed April 10, 2024, https://www.huapala.org/Pul/Pupu_A_O_Ewa.html.

8. Kyle Kajihiro, "Mehameha Wale No O Pu'uloa, I Ka Hele A Ka'ahupāhau: Lonely Was Pu'uloa when Ka'ahupāhau Went Away," Fall 2017, *Biography*, Brown Bag Series, September 28, 2017.

9. "Kulāiwi" Larry Kauanoe Kimura, Kanakipila Records, lyrics and translation from Kamehameha Schools, accessed April 10, 2024, https://blogs.ksbe.edu/dabaker/2015/09/08/kulaiwi-larry-kimura-peter-moon/.

10. Mary Kawena Pukui, ed. and trans., *Ōlelo No'eau: Hawaiian Proverbs & Poetical Sayings* (Honolulu: Bishop Museum Press, 1983), 34.

11. Haunani-Kay Trask, "'Lovely Hula Hands': Corporate Tourism and the Prostitution of Hawaiian Culture," in *From a Native Daughter: Colonialism and Sovereignty in Hawai'i*, rev. ed. (Honolulu: University of Hawai'i Press, 1999), 136–47. First published 1991 by University of Hawai'i Press (Honolulu). Don Ho, among others, recorded a version of "Lovely Hula Hands."

12. Pua Case, "Ka'i Kūkulu," 2019, lyrics and recording at Pu'uhonua o Pu'uhuluhulu protocol website, accessed April 10, 2024, https://puuhuluhulu.com/learn/protocol.

13. Nā ʻAumākua, adapted from Davida Malo's *Hawaiian Antiquities* by Pua Kanahele-Kanakaʻole. Words and recording at Puʻuhonua o Puʻuhuluhulu protocol website, accessed April 10, 2024, https://puuhuluhulu.com/learn/protocol.

14. Pua Case, "Oli Kūkulu," lyrics and recording at Puʻuhonua o Puʻuhuluhulu protocol website, accessed April 10, 2024, https://puuhuluhulu.com/learn/protocol.

The Earliest Hour

At the bustling Manila airport, an older cousin, Arsenia, greets me with a touch on the cheek.

I first met Arsenia, then a young mother of two, on a trip to the Philippines when I was nine. That was thirty-one years ago.

In my young eyes, the country was a dizzying place—an army of kin, unspeakable heat, so many living in what appeared to be temporary homes, a patchwork of planks, wood, and aluminum siding. But I remembered Arsenia from the multitude of relatives in my family's photo albums. I remembered her simply because of the gap between this cousin's two front teeth.

Many of the other relatives, pleasant and quiet, receded from my memory, their images sealed in photo albums, only to be resurrected in my parents' conversations. Over the years, my parents would mention Arsenia's name, usually after receiving a letter in the mail written in a loopy script I found difficult to read.

Now, at forty, I am a teacher and a writer, and I have visited the Philippines a few times as an adult. Now my recollections are filled with the presence of adult cousins, their school-aged children, gray-haired relatives, and neighbors—laughing, shy, curious, and warm. Arsenia stitches me back to this place.

We depart Manila, going north, at the earliest hour. As the bus winds its way out of the city, the only sounds I hear are the alternating rhythms of grinding gears and squeaky brakes. Outside my window, lone, silhouetted figures—round-the-clock vendors, sleepless wanderers—emerge on the streets and sidewalks. Without the crowds and humidity that sweep in with daylight, the city becomes a muffled, languorous version of itself, as if immersed in the ocean. I fall into a half sleep in the lull, but not before noticing the changing blue light of night to morning.

Outside Metro Manila, the crown of the sunrise brightens fields of green rice stalks. Off either side of the wide, empty superhighways, a stark contrast from the city's older, narrower, thronged streets, signs of perpetual commerce appear—gardens and fruits for sale, pots of fuchsias and azaleas, watermelons stacked like pyramids under makeshift sheds. Beyond the dense city, merchants become pronounced as individuals, sitting and gazing at the sparse morning traffic.

In the morning light, the landscape reveals itself like a new planet, unoccupied and expansive.

Arsenia and I sit near the front of the bus bound for her hometown, Vigan, located in my father's native region in the north. For a short while, our bus follows a silver and orange jeepney that resembles, in its shiny extension, a rocket ship from a 1960 science fiction movie. Once the jeepney peels away, our bus trails another bus, this one impressively crammed with passengers, bodies like a solid wall in the aisle, pressed together on seats, arms dangling out open-air windows.

I glance at my sleeping cousin, who, at sixty-two, has grown fuller in face and figure. She wears a blue knit top and blue pants, like something my own mother would wear. Lost are the sharper angles of her younger years, yet her hair remains startlingly black.

Later, I will notice this feature in many members of her father's family, elderly people whose brown, wrinkled faces belie youthful black hair. I imagine special properties in their drinking water and consider Arsenia and these other black-haired elders as keepers of a hidden wellspring, a fountain of vitality. As I step into middle age, I am not here to pursue the secrets of eternal youth. Instead, I want to uncover the life force called memory.

Arsenia is the daughter of my father's only sister, Miguela. My father left the Philippines for the United States in 1928, settling into cannery work in Alaska. Some years after, he began sending money home to family, who often inquired in their letters for details of his new life.

How is America? Are the Americans nice people? Do you find jobs easily? Where do you live in Alaska? Do they need farmers like us there?

Arsenia had been a faithful correspondent on her mother's behalf. She asked her uncle in America, my father, for whatever financial support he could afford. *Manong Ben, I hope to become a nurse one day with your help.*

"He sent me money to continue my studies as a nurse, but I never got it," Arsenia recounts.

"What happened?" I ask.

"It was stolen at the post office," she sighs, the gap between her teeth barely visible.

Without the support, Arsenia could not continue her studies in nursing. She eventually married and had children. It is a happy marriage; she has a close, loving family. One of her daughters would eventually become a nurse and move to England with her family. I can't help but wonder what Arsenia's life would have been like if she had received the money. Born and raised in Southeast Alaska, I was a child of working-class immigrants. My family lived in a cozy two-bedroom home built by my father on wooded property six miles outside of town. Because we didn't have sanitation service, my parents burned our trash in an old metal barrel outside.

Though our family vacations in Canada, Washington, and California provided me glimpses of a wider landscape, we were far from affluent. However, it was my initial trip to the Philippines as a child that brought into sharp relief our different worlds: my privileges as an American—the material prosperity, the mobility, the opportunity—and the poverty and limitations of my relatives there. I came to understand more deeply the desire for this American dream.

Arsenia only recollects a dream. In her retelling of lost hopes, a regret, a what-could-have-been that I imagine to be: a career in nursing, a nice house in the United States, perhaps an American husband and American-born children, she stares out the window, the gap in her teeth barely visible again, and sighs. Time slips away. The dream fades quickly into the background, becoming a shadow of what it might have been. Arsenia remains steadfast in the present, resilient, and unwavering.

As the bus winds its way north, I spot roadside signs for Pizza Hut and Starbucks in the town ahead, and suddenly it becomes unexpected yet familiar territory. Fast food and pricey coffee franchises, the appearance of American taste on the landscape, the dream of an empire invading countless others' dreams long ago. An unceremonious presence of brands in America is for me in the Philippines an abrupt reminder of another life: convenience, disposability, abundance. I see it promised again outside the bus window: more fast-food signs, and more and more wanting the American way.

In their black sunglasses, our bus driver and his assistant look like the Blues Brothers, grinning and nodding to each other from time to time. Earlier in the journey, the assistant played B-movies in the small combination TV/VCR propped on a small shelf at the front of the bus. The films were mostly of the action hero variety—one from the Philippines, another from the United States, though I didn't recognize it—with the leads as a former cop and a renegade in a leather jacket. Six more hours to go on this over-half-day journey. We sink further into the vinyl seats, cool against the skin.

The driver stops twice: once for lunch and once for a cigarette break. At these stops, vendors parade down the aisle, selling peanuts in small plastic bags, hot dogs twisted around sticks, and corn on the cob wrapped in cellophane. I catch a whiff of the hot dogs as new riders board the bus. As a child, I couldn't wait for hot dog and cupcake lunches every Wednesday when Holy Name Elementary was in session. The school supplied the hot dogs while the mothers of each student brought in their (mostly) home-made cupcakes for the class on their assigned Wednesday. My adult palate hasn't strayed too far from my childhood's, but for now, I hold off on snacks and eat beef stew with stir-fried greens that Arsenia has chosen at our turo turo lunch stop.

"Do you remember Long Beach?" Arsenia asks as the bus proceeds toward the city of San Fernando.

I nod, reminded now that Arsenia was there too. She'd accompanied my family from Baguio, my mother's birthplace in the mountains, and where I first met Arsenia on my initial trip to the Philippines, to my father's native province of La Union. I wonder for a moment why I had this gap in memory before the memory readjusts. Seamlessly restitched.

When the bus arrives at the gray, sandy coast, I recall that first trip to the Philippines when I was nine. My younger sister and I played on the beach, flitting in and out of the water, thrilled to be cooling off instead of sweating like we seemed to always be doing in Manila. We whined incessantly about the heat, which so dismayed relatives like Arsenia. They called us spoiled American children. They compelled our parents to move the family from a relative's home with an electric fan to a hotel room with air conditioning.

The beach was a respite from our relatives and from the heat. My father stood knee-deep in the water wearing his undergarments—a white tank top and shorts. He gazed at the horizon. I looked in that direction too, wondering how far away we were from home in America, my feet sinking into the soft sand.

The bus passes a cream-colored one-story building with a red roof. A group of light blue uniformed boys mill about on the compound.

"That was your father's school," Arsenia points out.

He completed the third grade, dropped out, and eventually returned to trade school, at an age I don't know and will never know. My father was a boy who would always work with his hands: on the fields of California, in the salmon canneries of Alaska, in a hospital and a post office as a maintenance worker, and on the rocky coastline as a fisherman who taught his children how to tie knots for the lure on their fishing lines. Ours was a strained relationship of equally stubborn natures, easing only after I left home for college.

Bauang, Baloan, Bagar, Sudipan, Pagudin, and Santa Lucia. Each town we pass becomes a song in my head. Another B-movie on the portable screen. Another action flick. Is that Chuck Norris? I stopped watching a while back. Outside our window: a field of light green leafy plants springing from the earth like the raised arms of a congregation in prayer.

Then the field disappears. Outside our window: an old wooden house with shuttered windows, then a house of cement blocks, then a neighborhood of homes behind corrugated metal fences. Motorcycles zip around us, and we slow down behind the horse-drawn kalesas. Thirteen hours after our departure from Manila, we reach Vigan, where the sun is fixed in a sharp blue late-afternoon sky.

For the next week, I stay at Arsenia's modest home of rustic wood. I wake up to a rooster's crow, and the rooster never really stops crowing throughout the day.

Arsenia prepares simple meals of rice, meat, boiled vegetables, and camote tops ("Your father's favorite"). The family treats me to Jollibee one day for fried chicken. Her affectionate husband playfully shoos away the curious neighborhood children gathering at the open living room window or stepping into the house with their dirty bare feet to look at the strange visitor up close. I grin and wave at the giggling youth. I visit the museum and take snapshots of the old-world Spanish architecture of the city and its cobblestone streets.

Then, at my urging, Arsenia and I travel north to tour the region of Ferdinand Marcos, the long-time Philippine dictator. Growing up, I heard his name in my father's conversations with his friends. I was introduced to the words corruption and dictator. Though we don't discuss much politics, if at all, I gather that Arsenia and her family consider him a thing of the past.

When I learn that his body is being kept in Batac City an hour drive away, I have to go see for myself.

I study the body of the deceased leader on display in a glass case in a mausoleum. This Marcos appears in serene slumber, laid out in a white barong tagalog and black slacks, a wide ribbon drapes from shoulder to waist, and medals adorn his chest. Face to the glass, I study his jet-black hair and mannequin-like pallid skin. *This is a fake*, I think. Arsenia, who entered the crypt right behind me and viewed the body in speechless astonishment, has already left.

"Where is the real body?" I ask the tomb-keeper after suspecting the one before me is made of wax.

He laughs, his shiny, slicked-back hair unmoving, and replies in a slighted tone, "This is the real body."

I smile, concealing my disbelief. The word "henchman" comes to mind. I am mostly intrigued by how this dictator still yields power even after death and how the children of a deposed leader now hold political offices in the region. Soon, in future years, one son will hold the highest office in the land like his dictator father did. An enduring echo of power in a labyrinth with no exit.

We return south to Luna. I pay a visit to the church where my father was baptized. Soon after, we journey to my father's birthplace in the jungle.

By the following afternoon, as the scent of campfire fills the air and the occasional rooster's crow erupts on the roadside, our jeepney turns into the dense jungle of viny trees. The vehicle crawls up and down the dips of a dried-up, rutted road and parks in front of a string of small homes. I have a feeling of materializing into a different life, one that existed well before my own, one that had countless dreams, struggles, and celebrations, lived and returned, lived and died.

Trees and ferns reach for the sky, with large waxy leaves in the shape of long hearts and exposed roots stretching out and up.

We have arrived in Pitpitak, the literal translation of Mud-Stuck-On-Your-Shoe, my father's boyhood home from a lifetime ago. It is my very first visit. Fortunately, it isn't the muddy season.

Here, in this residence carved within nature, I am introduced to family members, raven-haired and dark-skinned, some serious, some smiling. At the lunch feast, they offer me kinilaw, a raw seafood dish, and this version with "jumping shrimp," the tiny, pink-shelled creatures wriggling and dancing like popcorn on the plate.

I am surprised by troupes of Filipino Boy Scouts who appear shortly after our arrival. We watch as these young ones pour out of truck beds and set up tents in a nearby cleared open field. This invasion of visitors doesn't seem odd at all.

Here, people play a game called Waiting. It is, in essence, a lottery. Someone comes around to collect bets and handfuls of pesos and writes down the player's special set of numbers in a small notepad: their children's ages, a wife's birthday, or numbers that inhabited their dream the night before.

The pool of money accumulates over a day or two or, if fortune has it, an entire week before the thick wad of bills finds itself in a winner's hands; the winning number is drawn from a shoebox full of torn and folded strips of paper. The money to be spent perhaps, among other essentials, on an evening of singing at the videoke machine under a small shack. The black night swallows my vision but doesn't obscure an imagined glimpse of my father's early life.

I see him catching shrimp in river traps, cool water swirling around his waist. I see him gathering firewood with a stoic look on his face, then playing with abandon in a makeshift fort with siblings. I see him walking along a muddy road to school, his footprints still visible on the terrain. In the distance, I can hear a young crooner's wavering rendition of The Scorpions' "I'm Still Loving You."

Malunggay Motherhood

On rainy spring days like this in Hayward, my mother cooks chicken tinola. Ginger and garlic steam rise from the pot, fogging her glasses. In her own bowl, she dips a spoonful of white rice into the broth, and shredded chicken and dark malunggay leaves float to the surface. I'm her child, so she feeds me first. "Subo," she says. She blows on the bite so that I don't burn my tongue. We eat together, me first and her second, always. Malunggay studs my spoon, and then it blacks out my front teeth. I smile like I'm toothless, like I'm a verdant green pirate.

***

Moringa olefiera is native to northern India, where it's considered the "Drumstick Tree" because of the shape of its slender pods. In India, the pods are parboiled and tossed into curries alongside coconut milk and spices, or they're mashed and lightly fried, turned into bhurta fritters.

In Philippine households, the tender leaves are eaten instead, tucked into soups and stews. I've never known the pods. The greasy bite of fritter, but oh, I've recuperated with so many malunggay stews.

***

After I give birth, it is all about milk. About how much I don't have for B. *Produce* is the word the pediatrician, the midwife, and the doula call it. "How is your milk production going?" they ask, like I am a dairy farm. No, not the cute kind with the cherry-red barn housing all of the hens. I'm the kind you'd find in the middle of Interstate-5 in central California, driving through the groves before you'd hit the herds of cows, glassy-eyed, sitting in the middle of dried mud piles, chewing on nothing because nothing grows underneath them.

***

I'm surprised to find my breastfeeding vitamin—the kind that's supposed to boost your breast milk supply—contains malunggay, or moringa. An illustration of the plant with its forest-green leaves in the shape of tears, the kind I shed in the shower while yelling at my breasts to work, do something, anything, goddammit.

I mutter the word "boost" under my breath and think of the handful of drops I save for B. The midwives and doulas call this "liquid gold," so I feel more pressure to hoard.

***

My doula, Karen, recommends the vitamin. When I give birth to B., I fall into quiet love with Karen. Of course, her name is Karen. Older white women named Karen who drive Teslas, smell of a mixture of lavender and (seriously) patchouli oil, and travel out of town for Renaissance Faires aren't really my type, but there I am, big-bellied, slow-dancing with Karen. Sure, slow dancing is a strategy to manage the pain, but my belly burns into hers, my head draping against her shoulder, and it feels like a middle school dance. The first slow dance I ever had was with a boy named Cesar, his hands burning on my hips. His fingerprints stayed there for the rest of the afternoon. My belly burns into Karen's, and I am certain that B. can sense this secondhand love.

***

My mom's here for a week when B. is about a month old. She eyes the vitamin bottle with the same suspicion she had for the value pack of coconut water bottles at Costco. "We did that first," she says with a huff. By "we," she means Filipinos. "And better. And how much did this bottle cost you?"

I don't tell her.

For a bottle of 120 capsules of More Milk® Moringa, $49.99. A bottle of 60 is $25.99. You're supposed to take 4–6 a day, which means a bottle of 120 lasts less than a month. In my desperation, I take a small fistful of them with breakfast.

I can already hear my mother's chiding: "Do you know how much malunggay you can buy with *that* much money?"

***

As a child, my mother used to sling fish to women walking their children to school before she headed to school herself. Her black hair was crusted in salt and scales. She stank.

"See, sacrifice," she says.

"But what about your other brothers and sisters?" I ask.

"I was the only one with enough business sense to sell entire baskets before school," she says with pride. "Plus, they didn't want to stink."

Malunggay grows so commonly that it is hardly mentioned in her childhood stories. She shrugs. "Of course we ate malunggay. It's basically a weed."

**

Mamay, my mother's mother, forfeited sacks of rice from her sari-sari store to occupying Japanese soldiers in their fishing village of Sorsogon. She once fled her home and accidentally left her infant son inside when the soldiers trampled through her doorway. She recalled that moment with a raspy chuckle. The question, "What kind of mother…?" underneath her own laughter.

But I wonder if starvation makes you forget your instincts. It makes you forget yourself. There were still fish in the ocean and in the river. "But all of those bodies floating…," she said. Between the choice to starve or eat, she quit eating fish, the most plentiful resource in her village, because she couldn't stop seeing the eyes of neighbors, people she'd once known, even the soldiers.

Mamay prided herself in her entrepreneurial spirit. She found a farmer who planted tobacco and convinced him to sell his harvest to her wholesale. She taught herself and her children how to roll cigarettes to sell to soldiers. She taught herself how to make soap, and the most popular batches she named after her two stepdaughters, Helen and Rosita. This was how she fed herself and her family.

**

I don't know much about my paternal grandmother, Lourdes, except that she died of lung cancer due to secondhand smoke before I was born and that she liked to bake chiffon cakes. How long did she stand behind my grandfather, an esteemed county judge known to be immune to corruption, before even her own children dismissed her as a lowly housewife? I want to know what kind of frosting was her favorite. Which flavor was in her imagination? Her world? What did she fixate on outside of her window on Dayangdang Street in Naga City, waiting for her children to come home, before the waft of golden crumb reached her?

**

I don't know how to catch or sell fish. I don't know how to grow vegetables except to stick seeds in soil and overwater them, then wait for nature to "do its thing." I don't know how to raise chickens or how to butcher them. I don't know how to bake outside of box mixes and canned frosting. I don't know how to roll cigarettes (without making them wet with my own saliva).

I don't know what it means to starve. I don't know if I have what it takes to survive motherhood like Mamay, Lourdes, and my mother survived (did they?) through war, famine, alcoholism, migration, and xenophobia as mothers and caregivers. Maybe they survived *because* they were mothers and caregivers, in community with other mothers and caregivers. I don't know what this looks like exactly, except for a bad Hollywood approximation.

In the early 1990s, my cousins and I gathered around my aunt's television watching the film, *Indochine*, starring Catherine Deneuve, Vincent Pérez, and Linh Dan Pham, about the fall of French colonialism in Vietnam. It's no doubt orientalist as hell, but all I can remember is the scene of a Vietnamese mother passing her child to another mother in her village. She lowers her shirt to reveal her chest and to feed this child that isn't hers. But the child is also hers, isn't she? She belongs to the village and, terrifyingly, optimistically, to the world.

My cousin commented, that's what Mamay did with my dad when he was a baby.

Does B. save me with her relentless hunger? Does her face rooting in my chest for nourishment I can't produce force me to be creative? I can feel the boundaries of my body being pushed to constellate with other birthers and mothers in that collective animal necessity to feed.

Someday, how will B. survive? Inherent in that question is, without me. What will B's survival show me?

***

So far, B.'s dependency on me teaches me how to fall out of love. Maybe it's less dramatic than that. How to draw my attention away from. Failing, one-sided friendships. My constant striving. My overcompensating. I just don't have the time for that.

***

I'm in the shower, a few weeks postpartum. Trace a finger along the linea nigra, the black line aunties tsk at, so this is one reason I was glad to be pregnant during the pandemic. But, oh, how I wanted all of those hands on my belly.

***

I'm binge-watching season two of *Bridgerton*, falling in love with Kate Sharma, the soon-to-be Viscountess of Bridgerton. Kate's blue top hat felt hunting against her deep brown skin. I want to rest my head on her shoulder. I fall in love with the postpartum doula, another woman named Karen. She's Cambodian and from Long Beach, and she picks up pork bánh mì and phở gà on her way to our house. I fall in love the instant her black hair drapes over B's squinting face. I fall in love with La Leche League volunteers on some cryptically named group chat on Facebook. I fall in love with the labor and delivery nurses who pick up the phone on urgent line weeks after I give birth. I fall in love with the members of "Milk 4 Milk" groups, which call to mind the brief encounters of Grindr but for milk exchanges and are arguably more intimate. Lactating birthers offer their excess milk, unregulated and for free, to those who aren't so lucky to produce for their children. They offer tidbits of traumatic birthing stories, their dietary intake, and if they've been recently vaccinated for Covid. Posts like: "I'm at Disneyland for the weekend. Just pumped 10 oz. Vegan; no dairy." "Arcadia. 40 oz of freezer stash. Hope to share with preemies!" "Fullerton, but can meet anywhere in OC. Just provide refill bags. My baby's on solids and doesn't need the milk anymore" populate the page. I heart each one and the requests and questions of each nonproducer. I fall in love with my own rage and depression and the way it so easily sheds from my body, like my black hair circling the shower drain. I fall in love with so many crushes and so many women, many of them mothers, that I can hardly stand the trembling in my arms and knees from the weight of so much feeling.

***

I'm an adult, and my mother is spoon-feeding me chicken tinola. "Subo," she says. "Eat." Malunggay leaves are caught in between my teeth, and I smile at my child, our toothlessness mirroring each other.

***

I fall in love the moment my mother cries after I plead for her to stay. I fall in love with her tears. I fall in love with her hands, plucking malunggay leaves from stems to place gently into my child's mouth. After my mother leaves, I get lazy, speed-pick leaves with both hands pursed, leave the stems inside some chickeny stew, and then realize how unwieldy and inedible they are, like even skinnier toothpicks. That's why there's someone whose primary job is patience—sitting at the kitchen table to gently tug leaves, one by one, from the rest, sustenance from the chaff.

Motherhood is like that, living in another time zone where the only way to prepare malunnggay properly is slowly, slowly, and with care.

***

I'm in the shower, letting the warm water sluice through that place I once called my pussy. I hear B. and feel my chest ache, and I wish the water were milk pouring through me. "Formula is okay," my mother begs. "It's what I gave you." Every day, I move closer to myself, even if no one else knows.

***

Finally, I fall in love with B. The blue birthmark is in the shape of a tear between her eyebrows. Her thick and black hair almost looks lacquered onto her scalp, except for the curls beginning to gather at the nape of her neck. Her eyes, nose, and lips—nothing like mine—were more aligned with her father's features. But when B. smiles in her sleep, she looks like his mother. B. is named after Mamay. There are so many mothers within her. There are so many who aren't my own and have never met or will never meet.

Her hiccups are a sign of her contentment. How full she is. And when she opens her mouth, all of that is green.

All of that green.

West Capitol Drive

Malunggay leaves are nutritious, routine ingredients in Philippine recipes. At colder sites of diaspora, where malunggay does not easily grow, the acquisition of malunggay leaves can represent comfort. Named for the photographer's home street in the Philippines, this series of photographs juxtaposes previously frozen, thawed malunggay against manila envelopes—central objects of immigrant bureaucracy—and against empty space. This series of photographs alternates between the frustrations of immigration and the central relief of preparing familiar food despite the distance from home.

West Capitol Drive, 2024, Photograph by Tammy David

West Capitol Drive, 2024, Photograph by Tammy David

West Capitol Drive, 2024, Photograph by Tammy David

West Capitol Drive, 2024, Photograph by Tammy David

West Capitol Drive, 2024, Photograph by Tammy David

The Disturbance

In the taut months after the forest guy disappeared, the usual quiet in which my life had passed assumed a certain solidity and weight, something that verged on pain.

I was 35. Like Rizal when he was killed via firing squad by the Spanish. Kafka when he became too ill to work and began to spend a lot of time in sanatoriums. But also like Flaubert when *Madame Bovary* began to be serialized. Sandra when she won her second *Survivor* season (the queen stays queen). Cristina Yang when she left Seattle Grace and moved to Minnesota. Van Gogh when he left Paris and moved to Arles. Neither here nor there in other words, a middle place. Like Dante the character when *Inferno* opens, midway through the so-called journey of life and alone in a dark forest. I could still see forest guy's forlorn face relaxing into a smile, the eyes shut and trying to contain, to disavow the mirth. Can still hear his laughter, which always began at the highest pitch, a berserk split-second ecstasy, before returning to earth. After which he'd recall something, a piece of information or surfaced insight expelled in a rush: ahhh, did I ever tell you— He was always did I ever tell you-ing: things about forests, things adjacent to forests, things resembling forests, things that didn't seem related to forests but somehow always arrived there after an excursion elsewhere. It could get exhausting—I was the earnest, nodding type—and a few times the mix of boredom and fondness was enough to lift me from the bed, and I'd move closer to him and hover threateningly and watch him look up, alarm on his face, before I leaned in for a dry, impromptu kiss. The next day, his limp body next to me, it'd be the hardest thing to peel myself from bed to get ready for work, even if that meant only a few steps to the corner of the living room that had become my workspace after they moved corp comm to remote. Then I'd make coffee for two, the smell his own cue to get ready to leave. *Did I ever tell you?* he would yell from the shower. I'd shake my head, yell back that I couldn't hear him, and check my calendar to see my tasks for the day. Our routine was gentle, unremarkable, nameless. So small and unassuming its vitality escaped me, how I was nourished by it. And so when, on a day when he was supposed to come over, he didn't, and I never heard from him again, the uprooting was similarly uneventful, congenial even.

That was in August. I remember because it was the same month my father died, and the whirlwind of burying a parent as the eldest child tended to drown out everything else—the odd combination of grief and logistics that at times conjoined in such vexing questions as did I want my father's hands on his side or together, fingers laced, on his stomach. Many families say it looks natural, relaxed, but also officious that way. Returning to the silence of my apartment after the cremation, I had the sense that I was supposed to be sad about another catastrophe. The hum of the city outside held no answers. I went to the kitchen to make coffee, and only while pouring it into my mug did I realize I had made enough for two, and I remembered.

All of this is my roundabout way of explaining why I must have welcomed the mysterious knocking at my door that began soon after. Soft taps, three sets. Tok-tok-tok. Tok-tok-tok. Tok-tok-tok. At around two in the morning, like clockwork. The first few times, I rushed to the door, curious, only to find nothing there—just the empty corridor, the building's splotchy beige paint job, and the sallow lighting that gave the walls and marble floors a sickly pallor. Then I stopped checking and just let the moment pass. I didn't mind ghosts, I told the usual people later that week. I could use the company. Their laughter was limp with unease—it must be tough to hear someone make light of his misery, the supposedly blinding grief. One said knocking was a gesture of politeness, warmth, or even someone seeking permission. ("Are these Malay ghosts?" "Austronesian maybe?"), and I should tell them to go ahead, come in, come in, just take a seat wherever. One suggested leaving some detergent powder by the door so we'd know if our knocker would leave a mark (and what if we get hooves? another asked). The rest were thrilled and recalled similar encounters in childhood homes, university dorms, and old hospitals in faraway islands. The words benign, benevolent, and cute were thrown around. Well, you need to report it just the same, one said, the stickler for the rules in the group, whom we sometimes joked was secretly in the government's employ. Finding no reason to say no, I said fine.

The corridor smelled like fried fish again was my first thought that morning. I used to find it charming—the familiar waft from a lived-in place, the comfort of a deep-fried thing—unlike the healthy, odorless insides of the condos that enswathe the city (like a forest! exclaimed the voice). In the high-rise where I lived for five years, I saw the person who lived across me exactly once, a mortifying moment one morning during lockdown no. 7 or 8 when we opened our doors at the same time, and our tiny overpriced studios briefly mirrored each other, an intimacy that we quickly tried to unsee. It must have been one of the drills, for fire or earthquake, mass shooting or insurrection, and I had no time to check the vicinity before I stepped out. Here, the smell of scalding oil went well with the building's old, homely energy, the sluggish, nervous pace by which things moved and unraveled: the residents, the bureaucracy, even the elevator that creaked as it now welcomed my weight (doors closing, warned the recorded robot voice). Despite being alone, I half-expected the strident alarm that sounded at every breach of the ridiculous 400-pound, three-person limit, a remnant from the first, toughest lockdown and a bane for the building's many senior citizens who routinely ignored the alarm, out of weakness or entitlement or both, as if saying they had all the time in this loud world. I watched the red numbers finally blink to G. On the ground floor, I crossed the short driveway that led to the spacious, unkempt parking lot at the back. On the other side, the guard on duty, the one with the Garfield eyes who always looked half-asleep, looked up from his phone and, seeing me, smiled and opened the door to a small office.

I was welcomed by endless paper inside, some in freshly trawled piles and others in calcified-looking columns. Yes, sir? a tired, chirpy voice called out from somewhere. How'd she see me? I looked around and caught my reflection on the full-length mirror to my left, right by a plastic desk on which loomed several of the aforesaid paper towers. Hello, I responded, unsure, my voice seemingly absorbed by the clutter. The first time I came here, I was turning in the required year's worth of postdated checks, for which I received the notarized lease agreement and the keys. I have something to report, but please don't laugh, I said. I must have heard someone chuckle, because I laughed, too, on instinct, until I remembered the state of things in my life, and the phantom smell of the forest guy's shirt upended my smile. I could hear the rustling of paper, which told me to wait, be patient. Nothing much has changed here. Since that first visit, I had come to this office a few times for all types of transactions: to get a permit every time I needed to bring up new furniture to my then-unfurnished one-bedroom unit, to request the installation of new fiber optic cables for the internet, and to coordinate the transfer and renewal of my quarantine pass from my old condo. There is now a standardized form for these things across all shared housing situations, a convenience if only they didn't have to be filled out in pesky triplicates, one for the resident, one for the building, and the last for the new government task force for so-called holistic post-pandemic recovery. When the building admin finally emerged, arms weakly akimbo, and asked how she could help me, I cleared my throat but was again struck by the silliness of what I was about to say. I smiled preemptively to let her know that I was aware of how unbelievable this sounded. I knew. I wasn't crazy. Okay, she said, tone neutral. Here it goes.

When I was done explaining, in the lull during which she was probably choosing between filing what I just reported or calling a mental institution, the alert to breaking news drifted inside the room. These days, as things stood, we knew better than to ignore such things, so we stepped outside. The guard and the building's maintenance crew were gathered around the small television. Onscreen unfolded the now-predictable sequence of footage: a blurred body splayed on a bloodied pavement, the disheveled face of a shell-shocked relative, a stoic policeman answering a reporter's question. That's two streets away, someone said. The anchor returned and dispensed a summary. Cops manning a quarantine checkpoint had fatally shot another one, a thirty-three-year-old ex-soldier who allegedly tried to pull a firearm from his bag amid shouted orders to go home. My hand went to my pocket to check my quarantine pass, which had become second nature after the fourth lockdown, when it was announced that the requirement would remain in place. The victim, the anchor went on, had been recently discharged from service after showing symptoms of PTSD, the medication for which was still hard to come by, despite the loosening of some lockdown restrictions.

How sad, the building admin said, walking back to the office. Anyway, about this knocking. Might it be a lost tenant who got off on the wrong floor? That always happens. Our senior citizens aren't remembering things the way they used to. Each time? I asked. I told her I had opened the door at first, and there was no one there. She appeared to think about it. So why report it now? And are you sure it was from your door? I was going to ignore it, I told her, but last night the knocking lasted beyond the usual moment and went on for two long minutes. Not only that, it came with a strong aroma, either cinnamon or a woodsy aftershave. Her eyes narrowed. Are you sure it's not the housewife from 607 baking the anxiety away? she asked. The barista from 606 said it's been a tough year for the housewife's Japanese crockery business. Huge during the pandemic, but people are out again and beautiful things are unimportant again. Also, they're so damn expensive. She chuckled. Anyway, if you're sure you want to report it—I gave her a contrite smile and apologized for the extra work, which she waved off—just give me a moment. I put my hand on a nearby pile of Manila folders. I'm sure there's no form for this, I said. The woman laughed. Oh, you jokester. Of course there is. There better be. She threw a glance at one of the CCTV cameras overhead. But we can just log it internally in the meantime if you want, she added after a pause. Not even sure where all this paperwork goes to be honest, she whispered. At this rate, I'm going to need an assistant just to keep up with the mountain of paper. Good thing so many people are looking for a job. Even the medtech in 401 lost her job recently. You'd think medical people are safe! Anyway, to answer your question, there *is* a form for Disturbances—she paused—but if I can be honest with you, the examples in the manual are nothing like this. Not even close.

11 Jan 2035
#120

Took a 'nap' after an early morning webinar and had a v vivid dream in w/c was walking around a Bangkok-esque place w/ J and O and J and was stuck in traffic of people and next to us a flatbed truck, also stuck, w/ a huge tiger increasingly getting restless and shaking loose from his leash and I was the first to run away (of course) and then shouting erupts and and police in full battle gear arrive and I duck behind a jeepney (so back to Ph somehow) and the owner of the now presumably dead tiger is mad and begins shooting at the crowd, and I wake up and begin typing this and just now remember that a webinar I caught early this week, on the history of the mangrove forests around Saigon, had a bit about tigers! And other wildlife! In the mangroves! W/c in the 50s the US forces—w/ their CIA friends fresh off their mission in the Ph—happily bombed. One participant, v movingly, shared that a group of middle-aged Vietnamese women, many widowed by the war that felled the mangroves and killed tigers, would go on to reforest areas of Saigon, moving around the same space where their husbands once roamed. A sort of trans-temporal reunification, the women bargaining w/ time, in the forest. Manila Bay ofc used to be lined with mangroves, too, w/c is still the case if one moved away from the gentrified area around the US embassy. Phantom mangroves! Phantom mangroves against empire!

***

The knocking could be a number of things. This I knew. Could be the wind, playing with a door's loose hinges. A neighbor loudly chopping some chives for a midnight stir-fry. Overtime hammering from a faraway construction site. Writerly hammering on a loud typewriter. Painful clack of high heels across the lobby's marble floors. Painful jabs on a punching bag next door. Someone two doors down playing car crash videos on YouTube to fall asleep. Someone's percussive laughter during a boisterous nightcap two floors up. Could be sex, someone's headboard taking a hit from rhythmic, patient, painful thrusts somewhere in the quiet building. Could be loneliness, the force of grief conjuring company—

The last one was suggested by a friend, in jest but, of course, also not untrue.

At least they weren't knocking during the day, which continued to march with blessed tediousness. After filling out the form, I received a square slip of paper that resembled a shrunken grocery receipt. Bare except for my complete name, the type of form, the date and time, and rubber-stamped with the name of our barangay ("So not bare?" piped in the voice). Back in my apartment, I put the slip with the others in an old microwavable container brimming with paper next to the bowl of aromatics and mess of keys on the fridge. I sat behind my desk and resumed the podcast episode I was listening to, which broke the silence and replaced it with the productive, much-missed white noise of a coffee shop or a Makati office.

The force of grief conjuring company.

I put an earphone in and hit Play on the video file onscreen, which unleashed garbled bursts into my ear and sent the figures inside the frame shifting in laughter. I was about halfway into transcribing this lengthy, meandering interview for a feature article. Two hours long, eight participants. All members of a farmer cooperative in South Cotabato who benefited from a special loan that a client—a mid-sized bank—had approved under a special lets-take-care-of-our-farmers-for-a-change program. As the laughter trailed off, I could see the three layers of bodies (two farmers up front, then two more rows of three) slowly return to their shy, stoic postures. I had forgotten what made them laugh. Someone's loudmouth wife calling them home to cook? A pun on their president's last name, Gagui? [Laughter], I typed. They were smiling at something outside the frame, something I couldn't see. Every now and then, bound at my desk like this for hours and hours, I'd remember that we used to actually be *there*. In the olden days (eight years ago or so), we'd wake up ridiculously early to catch a five a.m. flight to some faraway city, grab breakfast at the local Jollibee or McDonalds, then meet the people we interviewed for the content we produced. It was exhausting, of course, an hour-long flight for an hour-long interview, some nice (posed) photos, idle chitchat, a lot of work even before the writing itself. But when the annual report, brochure, or magazine feature saw the light of print, there was a sense that it was an actual thing you had done, a memory that involved actual people, conversation, and feelings (to advance a certain brand messaging or increase brand value, yes, but nothing was perfect in this mad world). Then the pandemic came, and they realized that (1) they could save tens of thousands of pesos on flights and accommodations by doing interviews online and relying on stock photos, and (2) very little of the things we used to exhaust ourselves for actually mattered (the big, catatonia-inducing lesson those first catatonic years). What was real, and what was real *enough*? It apparently didn't matter.

In the recording, one of the farmers mercifully returned to the story at hand, on the fighting that used to break out on occasion between rebels and government troops, the real, deep-seated neglect that made a lot of farmers angry and desperate, before finally, the president with the funny name interrupted, this special loan came along. Some sheepish smiles. Low-interest financing come planting season plus technical advice from an agriculturist, special rates for seeds and fertilizers and pesticides thanks to a tie-up with an agro-chemical giant, tiny crop insurance. So stable had the earnings been the last two cycles that they'd nearly amassed enough to finance the construction of the last stretch of road to the highway, no need to wait for government funds. Threshers and a storage facility are next, we've already identified the woodlot in a nearby forested area that we can clear—

That excited voice again: as farmlands sprawled, the forest gave way, nomadic versus sedentary, the story of the human race.

The history of the world, we might venture to say, is the history of forests.

I could hear my voice tremble in the recording and knew I was about to ask what my boss had called my usual woke curiosities, like, didn't it feel like you were doing the government's job, when the phone rang. This wasn't some gentle ring, but a clangorous muzak that I hadn't bothered to change since moving here. My laundry had arrived a few hours ahead of schedule. I went down to the lobby to pick up the bag of still-warm clothes and handed Ate Josie what I owed her, plus the usual tip. I was at the lobby again an hour later, this time to pick up the grocery I had ordered: the usual ingredients for the usual pasta, sardines and tomatoes, spinach, milk, paper towels, and a Coke Zero six-pack. By half past four, I was waiting to enter the Zoom call for the regular post-shift check-in where we reported what we'd done for the day and asked inane questions and got sucked into the whirlpool of endless small talk that always ended with reminiscences about the bygone era of onsite work. There was nothing out of the ordinary that day except whispers about yet another restructuring and possible layoffs. After the meeting, I shut my eyes until all the fake joy had dissipated from my face (ten minutes). Then I stood up, stretched, and walked to the bed, where I lay face down until some of the real joy returned (twenty minutes). Then half an hour of doom-scrolling and another half an hour to make the pasta. I took a bowl and the parmesan and chili oil to the coffee table at the center of the living room, where I sat, cross-legged, to eat.

Those days, I couldn't watch anything other than sitcoms or YouTube shows, mostly reruns, all perfect for mindless staring and opportunities for middling joy. I got a message in the middle of dinner from my mother reminding me of her meds for the week, and I transferred the amount to her caregiver with the usual perfunctory message (Ingat kayo dyan). I returned to what was onscreen, two drag queens talking about babies, and I found myself playing back a few times particularly funny moments (If you have a baby, you can't *be* the baby), finding some new tiny detail to observe each time, eagerly waiting for the funny quip, anticipating the eruption of laughter, then hearing that falsetto shriek and watching their faces crumple in sheer joy.

At the elevator the next day, the old man known on our floor for walking ghost-like up and down the corridors every morning gave me a derisive up-and-down look. The loud music and loud singing I can stand, he began, but playing something again and again for thirty, forty minutes? Blech! I blinked. That must be from a different unit po, I said. Thought I was going mad, he said. All that shrieking and laughter. Again and again and again. What a disturbance.

19 Sept 2035
#189

Just finished this book by an American anthropologist / missionary (ok, hold your horses) who spent years with the forest Teduray in the south in the 60s. Still thinking if I should include it. V affably told. And toward the end the author suffered through an epiphany so visceral he had a violent physical reaction to it. The way he described it—finding himself 'at the edge of a cognitive abyss' v reminiscent of that Vanessa Redgrave film The Fever, *in w/c the sheer contradictions of capitalist society convulsed through the protagonist's body and induced a delirious ... fever. It's the same here: the mind—or body—as site of seizure, its meager tools unable to apprehend the epistemic chasm, this time between a society built on egalitarianism, nonviolence, and lack of hierarchies and one premised on competition and insecurity (aka the market, curiously unmentioned). The 'fever' perhaps the imagination itself, structured a certain way, being broken toward a new paradigm, being given new eyes. The forest as this new set of eyes, a new apparatus of seeing. Cf* Sandali ng mga Mata *(#23).*

***

I had been to this city hall exactly once, just after college, to stand as ninong at the civil wedding of two friends, one of whom I was deeply in love with. A decade or so hence, the main building was still huge, imposing, and brutalist. The lobby pulsated with the usual chaos of people in vague queues to the metal detectors by the entrance, the elevators, the cashier windows, up and down flights of stairs, in plastic chairs, and conjoined steel benches. Once mighty signs (NO FACE MASK, NO ENTRY, MANDATORY TEMPERATURE SCREENING) had either been half-torn from doors or were yellowing faster than the aging plaster walls. Men in fatigues with long firearms slung over shoulders and faces buried in phones idled everywhere. Some section or other was always being repaired or repainted. On banners plastered everywhere was the president's lopsided grin, around which snaked the government's long-running slogan, on the supposed newness of things, countries, and regimes, how we must all do our part.

It was calmer on the upper floors, and the corridors smelled like moth balls. The stale air was austere with bureaucracy. People milled about serenely or, like me, were lost and trying to hide it. In my bag was a slip of paper—*the* slip of paper—that I was supposed to bring to some office somewhere in this labyrinth.

The building manager had looked apologetic (but also curiously grinning) when she told me a couple of cruel-looking men had barged into her office and said that the erstwhile untouchable recovery task force was being audited; god knows why, and could he have some of the recently submitted forms. She suppressed her first instinct—wonder out loud who the hell this man thought he was—and found herself reaching for the nearest pile. My form was on top. Disturbance—one of the men mumbled after skimming the report. This ought to be fun. He took a couple of piles, then asked the other to write down the instructions (go here), plus the location of the office and the allotted time slot for our barangay.

Just before leaving for the next building, he smiled and said the consequences for not showing up would be dire.

I had to take a day off, which filled me with mysterious consternation until I realized that the last time I skipped work, I stood watch over my father's cremation.

The security guard on the seventh floor gave crystal-clear directions to the office, which flew off apace with my first tentative steps. A series of rights and lefts and slight lefts and slight rights, u-turns and yields, as if I were journeying into the recesses of an ancient cave system, not the seat of government of the country's richest city. It took me another fifteen minutes from the landing to the poorly lit corridor where the office was. There was another queue inside. Of course. I was 345 on the line, and they had just called 219, which, based on how quickly the line was moving, meant at least an hour of wait give or take. I was instructed to go to a separate waiting room, also stale and austere but somehow newly painted. Lines to me were frustrating but impersonal, and I had always taken pride in my ability to stay put even if things had turned brutal. You settle like lichen, as the forest guy had told me. It must have been a month before he vanished. He'd noticed that we had sardine pasta four nights in a row (his lease had lapsed and he was staying over for a week). I considered being offended, but he added that lichen was a sign of a clean vicinity, pristine air, etc. I looked around the living room, littered with his things. Clean? I asked, and we laughed. From the door of the new room, I spotted an empty chair at the back, where I resumed my proud, stolid rendezvous with waiting.

The internal alarm cultivated by years of anxiety woke me up just in time to hear 340–360 being called. We were herded back to the original office. The person next to me looked familiar, which perhaps made sense because this was the schedule for our barangay.

I was asked the following questions at the window, from general, said the man mid-yawn, to specific:

1. Re the reporting process, did you report the incident in a timely manner?
2. Was your report acknowledged in a timely manner?
3. On a scale of 1 to 10, did you find the process efficient, reliable, and responsive to your need?
4. On a scale of 1 to 10, did you find the cluster authority [sitio, zone, or barangay] efficient, reliable, and responsive to your need?
5. Re the reported incident, did the appropriate government agency (if any) address your concern?
   A. If no, did the cluster authority escalate the report to the appropriate agency? Explain. (Use an extra sheet if necessary.)
6. On a scale of 1 to 10, were you satisfied with the resolution of the incident?
7. Re the reported incident (Disturbance), is the nature of the disturbance related to the following? Check all that applies: (a) peace and order, (b) community

relations, (c) health and the pandemic, (d) education, (e) economic activity, (f) labor and other subversive activities, and (g) others (please specify).

8. Does the disturbance present a threat to the government's post-pandemic recovery program?

9. Does the disturbance present a threat to the security of the community and/or the country?
   A. If yes, what is your connection to the disturbance? (Use an extra sheet if necessary.)

10. Has the disturbance been resolved?

I thought hard about the last one and realized that the knock hadn't come the last two or three nights. Yes, I told the man. Yes. Yes.

Then I heard it. Soft taps, three sets. Tok-tok-tok. Tok-tok-tok. Tok-tok-tok. I looked around the murmuring office, feeling vacant and unsure. The bureaucracy hummed around me, the bureaucracy now metabolizing my noes and yeses. But the man seemed satisfied with my answers and told me I was free to go.

Instead of going home, I headed to my old college campus nearby, where I walked and walked under familiar trees.

*Michael*_____

It was getting near the usual time, shortly before midnight in the heart of Manila. Fear, like ice, coursed through her limbs.

Still, Lizette del Mundo Cruz had yet to gain back even a fourth of the weight she had lost in the first six months that she was haunted by Michael's ghost.

These nights, he appeared once, maybe twice a week. But not knowing exactly when he might arrive had blighted Lizette with insomnia. She could do nothing in the dead of night but write and wait. She would wake to his stark, frigid presence in her room, his silent words of accusation, and his malevolent glare.

During the day, Lizette suffered an extreme loss of appetite, so that a plate of even her most cherished food held not the slightest allure.

Now at a wraithlike ninety-eight pounds for her height of five feet, four inches, Lizette looked like the living dead. A popular political blogger and among the top opinion-shapers in the country, she had transformed seemingly overnight.

"It's too much. Stop it!" family and friends exclaimed, aghast, as though Lizette had chosen this transformation, as though she could stop it. Yet she couldn't tell them why. Who, in their right mind, would believe the truth?

That deep in the night, every single week for the past year, the dead came to torment her.

Lizette shuddered, and then she sighed, resolving to channel her resignation. It was an attempt to tame her fear, cloak it, or soak it somehow in the protective cynicism that had always been her recourse.

Yet it was those first few moments that always seized her by the heart, grabbing hold of her throat with frozen fingers, choking the courage out of her, rendering her mute. The sheer dread in anticipation of those first moments was more stupefying still.

She tried to expect the worst of it, training her heartstrings and trying to accustom them to the most unspeakable sights. But always, she failed.

"Mind over matter," she murmured to herself. "This is just a movie. This is a TV show. This is a nightmare." But it was of no use. Her fear was more real than anything else in her life.

Every time she saw him—even when she caught just a glimpse of him, it didn't matter how many times—it was always as though it were the first time. And then, in dizzying fashion, she was stricken, helpless, dumb, and numb. Michael surprised her, accused her, and mocked her. And then he spirited her away to the poorest districts of Manila. Places where everyone purchased pagpag at ten pesos per half kilo. Accumulated leftovers from the refuse of city restaurants were reseasoned and re-cooked over the highest heat in an attempt to kill the bacteria.

Tondo. Baseco. Payatas. Pasay. San Andres. Sta Cruz near the cemetery. Bagong Silangan in Caloocan. Bulacan.

Once there, she saw killings. In one night, as many as twenty-one deaths occurred. Bullets riddled bodies repeatedly; bodies writhed before her in agony before finally juddering silently. He made her witness hundreds of thousands of executions, some by masked men on motorcycles, many by policemen.

And it would not stop. Lizette was forced to behold virtually everything she had categorically denied multiple times, in print, online, and out loud for months and months.

How killers, on orders, reached into their pockets to plant evidence from a seemingly endless supply of identical plastic sachets of crystal meth, scattering them amid the still-panting bodies post-deed.

Michael made her see the way small firearms were placed in their dead hands for the photos. And then, carefully, the men would take the planted weapons back, wiping them off with old newspapers.

She saw the dead the way she saw Michael each night, in flesh and blood.

She smelled them—their dank mix of wet mud, piss, blood, and rot. They brushed against her, running through the steaming chaos amid wriggling, scampering rats, flying cockroaches, and bats. Hot tears streamed down their stiff, gray, blue-green-bloodied faces. They flailed their arms and wailed in her ears for their wives, their children, and their parents before dissolving in deafening, unintelligible groaning and screeching.

At some point in every night, one or another would make eye contact with her. It would hiss and scream with unexpected recognition. Once, it was a cadaverous man with one eye. Once, it was the toddling corpse of a bleeding, blue-faced baby girl. Michael would grip her with a cold hand.

They knew her. They read her. They saw what she had thought of them at one time or another: that they were no one. They were nothing. And in that chilling second that seemed to last a lifetime for Lizette, they paused in their wailing, stared her in the eye, and spat in her face.

Each time, something was always a bit different. A bit more gruesome. There was nothing that would ever allow her to relax in jaded recognition.

A babbling youth, tears running down his cheeks, turned to blood. A mummy in bloodied masking tape was limping toward her. A woman, eyes and mouth ringed with blood in a permanent mid-bawl, hands shielding who? Protecting what?

These night visits would always end with Lizette in a dead faint. She would awaken an hour or so before daylight, breathless on her own sheets, drenched in a pool of her own sticky, clammy sweat. The heady stink is still hanging in the air. The dirt and the blood of the dead were drying on the soles of her bare feet.

It had taken all of four nights before Lizette began to shift the timbre and nuance of what she wrote. Now she was less simplistic, less certain, less judgmental, and more complex. Now, she approaches compassion.

After seven nights of terror, she began to acknowledge and concede the counterarguments of those who criticized the "drug war." She began arguing along with those advocating for the families of the victims—those who cared and worked to protect the rights and very lives of the endangered destitute.

Lizette began to write with feelings for the victims of mistaken identity, for the children who were "collateral damage," for the former users, and for the users themselves. After all, she had seen the heinous acts and the malicious seizure of these lives.

Her allies attacked her, accusing her of turning "yellow." Her readers complained that she was being paid for this conversion; it was the only explanation. Instead of admiring congratulatory mail, she now got hate mail and death threats.

She wanted to tell them, "Look at me. I die every night."

She began to volunteer with a few underground church groups, people who were working to raise funds and help the families of thousands of helpless victims, knowing there were so many thousands more without assistance.

After two months, she began to write about the depth of corruption in the Philippine National Police. She composed a particularly bold missive to the president, pleading for him to see that his own words had undermined him and his drug war from the very start. This letter raised the ire not only of the administration's ardent supporters but indeed of the office of the president itself.

"Among the choices, he was perhaps the best choice. But the cruel and abusive methodology of his drug war is the result of his own impulsive tirades, his tremendous error in judgment, the paucity of his reason, and the condoning evil of those who are closest to him. By the president's own admission, the drug problem is unsolvable. Why, then, should the poorest of the poor continue to suffer this abject cruelty? Growing up without their parents, who are forced to work overseas due to lack of jobs, so many impoverished children succumb to drugs as a remedy. The poor have suffered enough for decades, day by day and year by year. Do they deserve to be killed by the very forces who are supposed to serve to protect them?"

Lizette no longer recognized herself in the mirror. Not the hollows beneath her eyes, not the crevices below her cheeks, nor the jarring boniness of her shoulders and arms, nor the sharp angles in her clavicle.

And what of her followers, all her kindred spirits? They no longer recognized her blogs, tweets, and posts.

What on earth had happened to Lizette del Mundo Cruz?

Lizette smiled wryly at her reflection, practically a skeleton of the woman she once was. Ah, but wasn't losing weight a good thing?

She peered dully into the glass to examine the grays of her eyes, but was all of a sudden distracted by a shape-shifting flicker behind her. The sight of Michael's disembodied face by her shoulder, burgundy-blood-stained as on the night he was shot two years ago, trapped a shriek in her throat.

Lizette turned to see nothing at all behind her. She whimpered when he was in the mirror once more, now speaking to her.

"No, it's not a good thing at all! You look like a drug addict. You better eat or you could die." Michael said with a grin. But the ghastly smile never reached his dim, tortured eyes.

And so it happened that night, as it had happened on many nights.

But sometimes, every now and again, a different Michael came. Not Michael the pedicab driver and drug user, mourned by his beloved.

No, once in a while, it was Michael Briones, the journalist, that appeared to Lizette.

She felt cold anxiety mixed with regret and longing.

Where Michael brought Lizette to deadly places, Michael Briones transported her back into the deep, unknown cavern that was her own heart.

She and Michael Briones met when they were fellow writers at school, both of them from the same large provincial city in the south. For a time, they were lovers, and Lizette had believed they might one day even be married. But after graduation, he returned to their hometown and worked for the daily paper there. She stayed in Manila and got a job in communications.

They quarreled frequently and grew apart, and eventually, the strain of distance and their own differences simply proved too much. They broke up like a glass vase, shattering upon a cement floor.

Years later, Lizette heard that her ex-boyfriend was shot by unknown assailants, killers on a motorcycle riding in tandem.

Michael Briones's murder remained unsolved, as so many murders in the country do. But those he worked with at the paper believed his investigative reports on the drug trade became too much for those in power.

Some nights, Michael Briones came to Lizette in her bed, and somehow she forgot he was dead. She forgot they had ever parted ways, and she remembered only her heart's joy in him—the truth she kept hidden even to herself: that she loved him and would only ever love him.

Michael Briones would reach for her and caress her. They would make love. But somewhere through that, just as her desire was most pining, he would pick a quarrel the way he always used to. Their bare limbs still intertwined, and he taunted her.

"Your problem is hubris, Lizzy. You always think you're right, but you're wrong. Dead wrong."

And then Michael Briones would roll over, and she would see his face ripped and ruined by the bullet that killed him, leaving him bleeding and broken, his eyeballs protruding from their sockets. Lizzy would scream and scream over his rhythmic, methodical chanting.

"Dead wrong. Dead."

Lizette wondered how long she would have to bear these ghostly burdens. She could well die from them. She wrote more, wrote harder, and more critically about the tragic events that were coming to bear upon the country.

Instead of leaping to the usual, partisan conclusions, she began to doubt her own impulses, even her own thinking. Now she spoke with everyone. She asked them many questions. She kept her mind white, blank, and open like a piece of paper instead of already having the outlines drawn in. She tackled issues of governance and separated personalities from policies and politicians from principles. She kept tabs on her old allies, even though they hated her, and she made new ones. She always revealed the new issues she continued to discover regarding the president, his family's corruption, and the company of plunderers he kept.

And then, first one and then another of her fellow ardent pro-admin bloggers began rapidly and abnormally losing weight.

They appeared at political events with dark circles cut deeply around their eyes. Lizette noted their changing appearances, recognized what was happening, and sensed the tides beginning to turn. Like her, they grew gaunt and hollow-cheeked, and like her, slowly, they began to question and criticize. Truth began to rise to the surface, just like the bodies of dead drug suspects, once deliberately weighed down with stones, now jostled adrift by currents.

Never, not even once, would Lizette acknowledge her role in the initial and then rapid decline of the president's widespread popularity. His once-soaring approval ratings sank, precipitated by the shifting rejection from his own supporters. Their fervor for the "drug war" was the lynchpin of loyalty that no one believed would ever wane. But then it did.

Lizette continued to work for the country she loved, and unlike before, she became respected by those who knew her and worked with her in the weeks, months, and years that followed. Change had come to her indeed. She was never the same again.

She would, of course, confide in no one that long after Michael disappeared, finally ceasing to torment her nights. Michael Briones instead would descend once, sometimes even twice a month. And always, in the same way.

In those fervent encounters, she feared for a split second that moment of reckoning as he turned mid-caress to face her. And then she sighed with relief and rapture to find his beloved face awaiting her kisses, whole, happy, and alive.

Radio Kiss Kiss

It took the crate twenty-four hours to travel by freight train from the Philadelphia Battery Company to Grand Central Station in New York City, where it spent a couple of days in a concrete warehouse a block away on Madison Avenue, then another four months via the Allan Line Royal Mail Steamer cutting through Panama, then northward to San Francisco, before finally sailing west on the Pacific Ocean to its final destination, the American colonial territory capital of Manila. Once there, it was unloaded on the frenetic pier at South Harbor, among towering stacks of produce to be exported out and manufactured goods to be imported in—for this port had been the busiest in Asia since the turn of the century—and remained a short while in one of the hulking customhouses at the mouth of the bay while the Insular Collector of Customs ascertained and verified its duties, and was then transported by narrow-gauge railway to one of the houses of the Customs Arrastre Plant. It would take another week for it to move on, hauled by truck through centuries-old cobble-stoned streets, then winding down narrow passageways along the languorous Pasig River, whose jade-green surface slowly lifted in the wake of drifting canoes. Thereafter it meandered through the business district, past Ford and Packard automobiles jostling for precious road space with obsolescent but practical horse-drawn *caretelas*, following the route of the fifty-three-year-old *tranvía* still tenaciously snaking along its silver tracks, and onward through one of the many dusty paths that extended like antennae out of the ancient walled city and into the new incipient suburbs, where large wooden houses still redolent of the Spanish *"tsalet"* style dotted interminable stretches of rice paddies, one house a good distance from the other, and where the fertile clay and loam far enough from the coastal salt air had proven beneficial to gnarled and stately sugar apple trees and young tamarind shrubs. And only after this epic, impossible journey did it reach its intended recipient, a modest but fairly commodious two-floor wood-and-stone house on the slopes of a hill in the district of Sampaloc, where it would be carefully dismantled to reveal its precious cargo on a searing tropic afternoon that would remain, to the young girl who witnessed its unfolding, the most memorable of her life.

Adelina couldn't get enough of Glenn Miller, and the only person she could talk to about it was her Aunt Nelia, her mother's cousin who lived in the city, and who she called every day on the phone to gush about what Aunt Nelia teasingly called her "crush."

But it was more than that. It was an obsession. Radio KZKZ was all Adelina could think about the minute she woke up and even after she said her prayers at night, and *In the Mood*, which the station played every hour on the hour, kept spinning in her head even in her sleep.

As she recalled later, Adelina thought the day they unpacked the Philco cathedral radio marked a crucial turning point in her life. As its name implied, it seemed to her like a house of worship, clad in a chassis of mahogany so polished she could see her reflection on it, its speaker reminding her of the stained-glass windows of basilicas she only saw pictures of in the pages of her mother's Bible, from which choirs of angelic, if modern, voices emanated, summoned by some divine power, and all she had to do was turn the chestnut-brown Bakelite knobs to invoke their majesty. How marvelous it was to be transported to some paradisiacal dominion by nothing more than sound.

She wasn't always prone to such dramatic pronouncements, but the radio was a rarity in her part of town, which at that time was so bucolic and so far from the city center that a proper marvel of new technology was the last thing you'd expect to find in a house as "old-fashioned" as theirs. She was careful not to use that phrase when describing the house or even the neighborhood in front of her mother, whose thin brows crinkled to a frown every time she heard her say it; her mother had been persuaded to move here a couple of decades ago by her late husband Cristiano, who had been convinced the city would soon extend its borders to the far-flung suburbs, which were the site of the future he, just like the many young men of his day, personally believed he could foresee. But from the moment they released the radio from its cumbersome prison where it had endured its marathon passage from America, miraculously unscathed from the ordeal, gleaming as the day it had rolled out of the factory, Adelina decided she would be called by something as new, as modern, as catchy as the magnificent contraption that instantly became the centerpiece of the house.

"From this day forward," she declared, "my name is Del."

Aunt Nelia loved it. She had a program at the radio station herself, one of the few that Filipinos were allowed to produce and air. It was a variety show where she told tales, sang a few local songs, and quickly garnered an army of fans. Del, she said, was a radio name, a performer's name, a name that people could quickly remember.

Her mother slowly began to get used to calling her by that name too, if somewhat reluctantly. Amelina had bought the radio as a gift to herself and her daughter. She could barely disguise her disapproval of Aunt Nelia's endorsement, much less her "profession," which she considered just slightly less disgraceful than the vaudeville performers in the city, and she didn't know much about radios or newfangled contraptions from America, and often, staring with a sinking heart at the monstrous machine, she wondered what it could really offer aside from the news, most of which was dire.

America had barely come out of the throes of the Depression, when people were starving and out of work. But it wasn't felt as keenly on these islands, and Amelina wondered if they were so far away that even the vicissitudes of economics could barely touch them. She still had a steady stream of income from the stocks on which she had invested her husband's life insurance. He had died ten years ago, which seemed like a very long time but which she relived each time the dividends came through—relief shot through with pain. There was also the rent she collected from various properties in the city, which gave her enough money to save up. Purchasing a radio was the only concession to her newfound wealth that she allowed. It had cost all of twenty dollars, which at that time was a lot of money, and adding the shipping costs and taxes, it was an extravagant splurge. In all other matters, she remained frugal and discreet.

"People who flaunt their wealth are vulgar," she often told Del. "And don't let that radio take you away from your prayer meetings. I've been told you've already missed a few."

She had enrolled Del in a study group of girls the same age who met every weekend at the parish church to learn new prayers but mostly to talk about boys and radio, two topics that not surprisingly consumed them. When they learned that Del's mother had just bought a radio, they couldn't wait to let her tell them all about it. She talked about her favorite station—she called it Radio Kiss Kiss, which sent the girls tittering—and shows like *Klim Musical Quiz* and *The Listerine Amateur Hour*, and she hummed Glenn Miller to them, and together they improvised dances to the music, going back to their solemn prayers only when Father Jose, the parish priest, walked in.

Amelina soon learned that Radio KZKZ broadcasted from the Heacock Tower, in the business district of the old city, where Cristiano had died. A feeling of dread came over her. She imagined the signals pulsing from some imponderable origin and wondered if the static they often heard was the garbled speech of lost souls. It didn't help that all she listened to was the news on Voice of America, and all the news was about the possibility of Germany starting another war in Europe. She began to regret that the radio was a nagging testimony to a bad decision and eventually acted as if it were merely another piece of furniture and not one of those fashionably new contraptions the city was fast embracing, and its position in the sala, bulky and commanding as it was, was simply a reminder of some lapse of reason she would have to live with for the rest of her life.

And so, it was Del who listened to it all day long. Anything so novel, her mother conceded, was better left to the young. Del feared her mother would come to her senses and resell the radio, and she prayed every night for the good Lord Jesus to save it from such a fate. And in the dead of night, pretending to be asleep, she would hear her mother at her nightly prayers, mostly for the soul of her late husband, whose youthful portrait sat on an altar right next to that of the Sacred Heart, fortifying her with the thought that he was constantly looking over her shoulder, keeping watch on the fragile world that he had left too early. Del would then hear her shuffling out of her room to check the windows and doors, as was her custom, and eventually stopping in front of the hulking apparatus, and always, thinking no one else was awake, Amelina would tune in surreptitiously, turning the dial gingerly with the tips of her fingers, frisking through the music, and stopping only when she finally heard news about America and the tenuous predicament of Europe on the brink of war. She would have taken comfort in the thought that, indeed, they were so far away that war was not even a possibility, especially when America was doing all it could to avoid getting involved. Del could hear the soft murmur of the newscast as she drifted to sleep, and in that state that was not quite sleep and not yet dream, she imagined her mother thinking exactly the same thoughts she had, that it was an extraordinary world out there, vast and unexplored, one never before imagined, and in those quiet hours they, mother and daughter together, separated only by the walls of the rooms, opened their own small world to let that other realm in, new and mysterious, but wondrously accessible and real.

***

Every weekday morning, Amelina and Del walked down a few blocks to the school, where Amelina taught English and Del was in sixth grade. Del loved coming to this school, which occupied a full block along a street bustling with horse-drawn *caretelas*. The building had been designed just over a decade ago by the brother of the famous artist Juan Luna, with its portico of stone balusters, mother-of-pearl window panes, and mansard roof with small gables and dormers. It was like entering a different city—elegant, refined, and thoroughly American—the very epitome of the new era that was just in its prime.

They would always enter through a garden lush with bougainvillea and jasmine boughs that overhung the cobble path. Mother and daughter strode into the building side by side, and at the lobby, Amelina would head off left toward her classroom, leaving Del to walk the other way toward hers.

But what Del loved most about being there was the chance to see her girlfriends from the prayer group, who always waited for her mother to leave before pulling her over to a corner, where they spent the few precious minutes peeking out toward the boys' entrance at the far end of the campus.

"Mama would kill me if she ever saw me doing this," Del always protested, but even she couldn't help delighting in seeing the boys brazenly waving at them.

"Who do you like the most?" one of the bolder girls, Jenny, always asked them. Her real name was Eugenia, but no one called her that anymore, and all the girls had always known her as Jenny.

"They all look too young for me," Del would always say.

"Give them a couple more years, and they'll be dashing and handsome like Father Jose at the church," Jenny would reply, sending the group into more giggling fits. But turning more serious, this morning Jenny said, "Your mother keeps you on a tight leash."

"Does she?" asked Del.

"Yeah," said Jenny. "Your skirt's too long. You look like an old lady." She reached down and folded Del's skirt up an inch.

"Don't you dare, Jenny!" Del protested. "I don't want those boys to see my knees!"

"Spoken like the nun she was raised to be," said Jenny. "You'll wind up looking like those girls from the backstreets of the neighborhood. Downright dowdy and poor."

"That's not a nice thing to say," said Del.

"I know," said Jenny. "I'm sorry; I shouldn't have said that. Maybe we can donate your dress to one of them, so you can have an excuse to get a new one."

"Jenny, you are insufferable."

"Ah, another new word learned, eh? That's good. You and I will master the language and be better at it than the Americans. Then..."

"Then what?"

"Then we'll write our own poems and stories, and we'll take over the newspapers, and we'll show them Filipina girls are not to mess around with."

"Won't that scare the boys, though?" asked Del.

"The ones who don't get scared are the only ones that matter," said Jenny defiantly.

The bell rang, and they trundled off to their classroom. Inside, as they started their first English lesson, which was taught by Del's other aunt Dolores, Del couldn't help looking around at the other girls. Silent, obedient, docile, and, as Jenny had sadly noted, looking rather poor. She noticed that their hands, properly clasped on the desk, were rough, their fingernails clipped short but still showing dirt under. Their clothes were faded and threadbare.

Later that afternoon, Amelina came to fetch Del. They would walk home together, as they did every day after school, a ritual that Del was starting to resent because it prevented her from hanging around with Jenny and the other girls, whose parents were not as strict.

This afternoon, they saw Dolores outside on the school grounds, having a rather tense conversation with the school custodian.

"Diego, I told you to keep the grounds clean," Dolores was telling the man. "The students will catch something if there's any rubbish lying around." Dolores was the older sister of Del's late father, Cristiano. Perhaps because of the series of tragedies that had befallen her family, not the least being Cristiano's death at the tender age of twenty-nine, she had the air of a stern old maid, which in fact she was.

Diego Santa Ana, a gruff and scruffy man, replied, "I don't take no orders from no woman."

"Well, you must," said Dolores. "If you are to keep your job, and do mind your grammar, please."

"Someday we'll be in charge, and people like you will be taking orders from us," he said.

"Until that day comes, you must do as you're told," said Dolores, who saw Amelina and Del coming out of the classrooms and gave them an exaggerated shrug.

"Is everything all right?" asked Amelina.

"Diego refuses to do his work," said Dolores.

"I work so my daughter can attend your school," said Diego. "But I am not your slave."

The argument continued, and Amelina and Del left Dolores to sort it out. They walked back the same route they took that morning, side by side, slowly and in dignified silence. As they reached the house on the hill, Del noticed, not for the first time, how it loomed over the rest of the neighborhood, like an old castle or a sentinel.

"Your aunt told me you had trouble concentrating in class today," said Amelina.

"My classmates are all poor, Mama," said Del.

"I know. That's why I gave money to the school, so they don't have to pay to get an education."

"There's a girl in class that I feel so sorry for. Her dress is just all tatters, like she's wearing rags."

"What would you have us do?"

"Give her my dress."

"And what about you?"

"Nena can make me another. Nena would love that. She loves making things."

"Nena is here to do housework, not to make you a new dress when you feel like it."

They reached the front gate, and Amelina unlatched it and led the way in. She must have been thinking about what Del had just said, because as they walked up the steps to the front door, she continued, "All right. We'll give your dress to that girl. But you will wear the white dress you always wear to your prayer meetings."

"Oh, Mama, no! I would look like a nun!"

"Better a nun than…" Amelina was at a loss for words. But finally, she said, "Oh, Nelia has such an awful influence on you."

***

Del didn't feel like going to the prayer meeting the next day, but she knew she had no choice. To her surprise, all the other girls were wearing the same dress.

"We heard what you did for one of the girls in school," Jenny told her. "We all decided to do the same."

"We look like a gaggle of nuns," Del said.

"Crazy nuns," said Jenny. "Nuns no nunnery would welcome."

They all had a good laugh, but there was one more surprise waiting. Father Jose had heard about their good deed, and as a reward, he allowed them to use the piano in the sacristy for the day, but only to play devotional hymns. Since only Del and Jenny had started taking lessons, they took turns being the day's accompanist.

At the end of the meeting, when she was sure Father Jose was either back at the rectory or at least out of earshot, Del began playing the opening strains of *Moonlight Serenade*. The other girls recognized it, of course, and began dancing a waltz with each other. Jenny led them; she was the best dancer in the group. They swayed across the hall in blissful abandon, and Del delighted in seeing her friends show off their best dance moves.

When she finished playing the piece, she couldn't help herself and began pounding the chords to *In the Mood*. The girls exploded in shrieks of delight. They began to boogie, some better than others, with Jenny teaching them the proper steps. Step right, left, back, and twirl. Repeat until properly breathless.

Jenny then took her place at the piano and continued playing the piece while Del joined the others in dancing. She closed her eyes and felt as if she were being transported to one of those glamorous dance halls Aunt Nelia always talked about, the exclusive enclaves of the rich and beautiful, the men in tuxedos and the women in sequined gowns that glittered like a firmament of nictitating stars.

She was still swaying to the rhythm when the piano suddenly stopped, and there was total silence. When she opened her eyes, she saw all the girls staring at her skirt. She looked down. There was a streak of blood running down the front—a stark red stripe against cotton that just minutes ago had been virginal white. Jenny rushed to her side and put her arm around her shoulder.

"It's all right," said Jenny. "It's happened to us all."

Del was in tears as she walked back to the house. Nena's son Sol, a lanky boy just a few years younger than she, saw her at the gate and did something puzzling: he quickly turned around, keeping his head bowed, and remained so until Nena saw her stagger in and ushered her to the kitchen in the back of the house. There, she let Del take the dress off so she could soak it in hot water. Nena could have been barely out of her teens herself; she looked so young, and the fact that she had a son like Sol was hard to believe, but she had grown up in one of the hardscrabble provinces and understood a lot about matters that Del hardly knew, and she told Del to take a thorough bath, washing the blood off her legs and feet, and it was only after all those ablutions that Del finally made her way to the living room, where Amelina had been darning a shawl, pulling the needle and thread with such deliberate absorption that she seemed not to notice Del at all.

"I'm so sorry, Mama," Del said. "I've ruined my dress."

Amelina hardly looked up from her sewing and said, "Did Nena help you clean yourself?"

"Yes, Mama. Am I ill?"

"No, just early," said Amelina. "Way too early." She let out a deep, prodigious sigh. Then, more to herself as she did during her evening prayers, she whispered, "They grow up so fast. God help us all."

*Tell Me How*_____

INT. HOTEL ROOM—DAY

Someone inhales and exhales, nervous. A hand extinguishes a cigarette on a makeshift ashtray.

The person gathers a notepad, a phone, and a conference program.

EXT. HOTEL ROOM—DAY

Marty, Filipina American, early thirties, leaves ROOM 505.

Something in her face is haunted. Sober.

EXT. HOTEL COFFEE SHOP—DAY

Marty has a small reunion with her fellow weather scientist, GEORGE, mid-thirties.

GEORGE   Actually, last year, before Yolanda, I'm going to leave already.
But PAGASA appealed for me to stay.

MARTY   After what we saw up there—I mean. The country needs you.

GEORGE   Not according to this government! Months and months, no hazard pay. Until now, I still borrow from my father-in-law. At least in Qatar, the exchange rate is okay.

They pause and drink their coffee.

GEORGE   Your family's not here anymore, right?

Marty shakes her head.

MARTY   My dad died here last year. Cancer. My mom moved back to California.

GEORGE   Condolence. Maybe you can go to Samar one day. See your mother's side.

He gathers up his things to leave.

EXT. PAMPANGA STREETS—DAY

Marty steps out into a spacious street. She's back in the Philippines, but in a different city: PAMPANGA is a former U.S. military base suffused with the endless presence of its foreign colonizers.

INT. HOTEL—LOBBY—DAY

Marty returns to her hotel. She looks at a large sign that reads, "Filipino Resilience: The Filipino Spirit is Waterproof. Fordston Foundation, December 10–13, 2013." She despises it.

She stops and scans a giant display in search of someone's name.

INT. HOTEL—CONFERENCE ROOM—DAY

Marty and George sit on a panel together.

AUDIENCE   But knowing the history of storms in the region, why
MEMBER [O.S.] wouldn't the people evacuate? Aren't they pasaway?

GEORGE   *[trying to be polite]*
                   Well, there are several stakeholders for any—

MARTY   It is utterly foolish and shortsighted to blame the victims of a disaster. No one up there knew what "storm surge" meant. It was too English. It was a failure of language, in addition to so many other failures of people in power.

Murmurs in the crowd. Scattered claps. Marty looks through the audience, but she doesn't find who she's looking for.

INT. HOTEL—BAR—DAY

The conference is between panel sessions. Marty runs into the old Fordston alumni.

They're standing with LEAH, a beautiful Filipina woman in her early thirties. Leah clocks Marty.

BROCK   Albescuuuuuuu! You're late! You missed my keynote panel with the Ambassador!

MARTY   That's too bad.

SHERRY   So good to see you. Three years, damn.

VANESSA   How's—where was it, Iowa?

MARTY	Wisconsin.
VANESSA	Sorry, they all look the same to me. How was it?
MARTY	Wisconsin was, uh. Full of lakes. Grad school full of grad students. Sky full of...weather. *They nod awkwardly.* *Vanessa and Sherry look at each other, trying to decide.*
SHERRY	This is Leah, Leah, this is—
LEAH	*[knowing, warm]* Marty. Good to meet you. I've heard a lot. *Marty's discomfited but polite.*
BROCK	Hey, I heard you went up after Haiyan, damn, you learn anything useful?
LEAH	You went there? *Marty hides her horror, remembering all that she saw after Haiyan. She keeps a neutral face.*

INT. HOTEL—CONFERENCE ROOM—DAY

Sidney, Filipina American, early thirties, speaks at a podium about her research. She sounds confident and mature.

SIDNEY	What we should conclude, from the narrative of pediatric patients in Krus na Ligas, is that the language of their symptoms is not limited. Rather, we as practitioners should be attuned to a child's storytelling—

As Sidney speaks, something catches her eye. Marty is in the audience. Sidney continues without pausing.

SIDNEY	...in their verbal and nonverbal forms. Adults do not own the experiences of child patients, not even—and especially—their parents.

INT. HOTEL—DAY

At the end of the talk, some people file out; some stay to speak with the panelists.

Marty waits, but she sees Sidney leave with Leah's arm around Sidney's shoulders. Sidney locks eyes with Marty. Then looks away.

EXT. HOTEL—DAY

Marty goes for a run, sidestepping the stares and catcalls of onlookers. She runs too hard.

INT. HOTEL ROOM—DAY

Sidney and Leah tidy the hotel room.

LEAH	You want to know how it went?
SIDNEY	Uh, sure.
LEAH	She's nice, but she was distant. Guarded. Tired.
SIDNEY	Okay.
LEAH	Mahal. Are you okay seeing her again? *Sidney stands to meet Leah. Leah is tense, hiding her worry.*
SIDNEY	Am I okay seeing someone who could never love me the way you do? Someone who will never be anything who even remotely approaches the wonder of who you are? *She kisses Leah.*
SIDNEY	Why don't we go out for a bit? Before we head back home? *Leah kisses Sidney.*

EXT. PAMPANGA MALL—DAY

Sidney and Leah go to a mall, hand in hand. Sidney is patient and loving with Leah, but you can catch glimpses of her own tension as she thinks about Marty.

EXT. KARINDERIA—DAY

Marty eats arroz caldo at a local karinderia alone.

She clocks an old white man walking with a younger Filipina woman. Korean and Japanese businessmen negotiate for time from an older Filipina.

Marty leaves her food uneaten.

EXT. HOTEL—DAY

Marty sees George, the weatherman, off to the airport. They share a strong handshake.

MARTY	Stay hydrated sa desert.
GEORGE	Yeah. And you know, Martika. What we saw. Don't hold it in, no? Call me, if you want to talk. Kahit ano. Whatever it is. Better to talk. Don't let it consume.

Marty nods. But she won't call.

George pats her arm. He gets into a taxi. Marty watches him leave.

INT. HOTEL CONFERENCE ROOM—DAY

Another day, another panel.

Sidney sits in the middle row. Marty is in the back, like the way they were seated at their Fordston orientation years ago, in 2010. Except now, Sidney is sitting beside Leah.

INT. HOTEL—LOBBY—DAY

Marty hears excited reuniting. Fordston alums take a group photo outside the conference room.

BROCK   Albescuuuuuuu!

Brock motions for her to join. Sidney doesn't look her way.

Marty reluctantly stands beside Brock. She looks at the person taking the photo: Leah.

LEAH   1, 2, 3, smile! Okay, now wacky. Come on, be Pinoy.

The group groans but poses anyway. Sidney and Marty stay unsmiling.

LEAH   *[to Sidney]*
                  Mahal, so serious.

VANESSA   Dim sum, yeah?

SIDNEY   We leave early tomorrow –

SHERRY   Sidney!

MARTY   I can eat.

LEAH   And I can drive.
                  [to Sidney]
                  Come on. It's good to gather after an accomplishment.

INT. CAR—NIGHT

Brock and Marty are in the back seat. Brock is telling an animated story that Marty doesn't hear.

Marty glances in the rear view mirror at Leah driving and at Sidney, who looks straight through the windshield, still not really acknowledging Marty.

Sidney takes Leah's hand.

INT. FILIPINO RESTAURANT—NIGHT

Marty sits across from Leah, who is seated beside Sidney.

The other former scholars cut eyes at each other, knowing about the old love affair.

Sidney drinks straight whiskey. Marty and Leah drink bottled water.

MARTY   Sports medicine. So, like, PBA players?

LEAH   PBA, the Volcanoes, the Olympian boxers. It's a privilege to serve them.

MARTY   It sounds privileged. Sorry, I mean, it sounds like a privilege.

Leah smiles. She knows what Marty's doing, but it doesn't bother her.

LEAH   Sidney returns every weekend to the clinic at Krus na Ligas. Even with her schedule. You remember it?

Marty nods.

LEAH   I keep telling her, doctors need free time for self-care, but—

SIDNEY   There is something to be said—

LEAH   For community care.

Leah touches Sidney's face and smiles, proud of her.

The night goes on, good dim sum filling the table.

EXT. RESTAURANT—NIGHT

Pampanga at night: neon lights, busy streets full of expats with young Filipina women in tow.

Marty watches Sidney walk hand in hand with Leah.

VANESSA   [to Marty]
               You good?

MARTY   Yeah, great to be back.

INT. GERMAN PUB—NIGHT

The gathering's an hour into a hangout at a German-themed pub, with everyone except Leah and Marty getting drunk. Servers walk in costume.

BROCK	Buckets half off midnight til one!! *[to Marty]* Bucket for the road Albescu?

Marty ignores him. She stares at a nearby table.

A paid double date is in progress: a middle-aged white American man, a middle-aged Korean man, and two young Filipina women—one a bit older than the other. They look somewhat alike, and the younger one seems new to the scene.

LEAH	It's troubling, Marty. But it's survival, no? At least they can stay home; they don't have to be OFWs.
MARTY	That's an awful bargain.
SIDNEY	Well, it's easy to judge from the outside.

Marty gets angry. She tries to hold back.

MARTY	The outside?
SIDNEY	How many years have you spent here?
MARTY	Yeah, you sure sound like an insider—
SIDNEY	Or is it weeks? We've done years of med school here by now—
LEAH	Mahal—
MARTY	An insider, with your rich family and their servants at home? I guess buying three years of med school trains you in more shitty opinions?
SIDNEY	It's longer than two weeks after Yolanda, parachuting in and out of a disaster zone.

The table gets quiet. That was mean.

Leah stops herself from arguing against Marty. She touches Sidney's hand.

LEAH	Sometimes you need an outside perspective. It's true. We're privileged. We can get complacent here.

Sidney relaxes.

SIDNEY	Yeah. That is true.

Sidney looks at Leah, vulnerable now, needing her.

LEAH	It's late. We should get back to Manila.
SIDNEY	We should.

Obnoxious laughter. Marty looks: The younger Pinay grows more uncomfortable with the behavior of the foreign date she's with.

The younger Pinay tries to go to the bathroom, but the Korean man grabs her by arm. He forces her to dance. Sidney notices Marty noticing.

SIDNEY	Martika—

Marty gets up roughly. She looks in Sidney's face, then rushes to the other table to confront the men.

MARTY	She doesn't like that. You should stop.

The Korean man laughs and ignores her.

YOUNGER PINAY	Bathroom lang po—

Marty opens her wallet and tosses pesos at the men, hard. Some coins and bills hit them and fall.

MARTY	Here's your money back.

Marty hands more bills to the younger Pinay.

MARTY	You're free now to go to the bathroom. Or go wherever.

The younger Pinay is resentful and spits back in Tagalog.

YOUNGER PINAY	Stupid FilAm!

The younger Pinay grabs Marty's cash and storms out.

AMERICAN MAN	And you are?

They stand and approach Sidney.

KOREAN MAN	Why do you throw your money around?

Marty doesn't retreat. She stares them down. Brock approaches.

BROCK	Fellas, fellas…
AMERICAN MAN	I think she's telling us she's free for the night.

MARTY   Fuck you, rapists.

The American man splashes beer in Marty's face. Marty overturns his table; it lands on the man's foot. The Korean man throws a glass. A messy scuffle. Marty ends up on the floor.

Brock holds back the guys. They calm at his intervention.

BROCK   Hey fellas, whoa. Look, sorry about our friend; let me get your tab.

MARTY   Fuck you too, Brock.

Marty starts to bleed from her nose. There's a lot of blood. She touches the blood on her face, surprised. No one moves for a moment.

Sidney rushes to Marty and picks her up from the floor.

SIDNEY   Hold this.

Sidney helps Marty up, instructing her to hold two clean napkins to her face.

LEAH   Let me help—

SIDNEY   It'll take too long to get the car out, just get them back to the hotel?

The men and waitstaff complain to Brock. Brock keeps calming them. Leah watches Sidney rush Marty out.

INT. CAB—NIGHT

Marty rides in the cab, holding a bloody napkin to her face.

SIDNEY   [on her phone]
               Yeah. I think you should go ahead.

EXT. BAR—NIGHT

Leah's on the phone in the driver's seat. Her car idles with the Fordston scholars riding along.

LEAH   You know my shift starts early.

SIDNEY   If this runs late, I can commute.

LEAH   Mahal. You know my lines. You're at one of them. I know she was important to you, but—

SIDNEY   She's—you don't have to worry. This—this is an old story. I love you. I love you.

Leah sighs. She hangs up.

VANESSA   Are they okay?

Leah doesn't answer. She starts driving.

INT. CAB—NIGHT

Marty sits far from Sidney, lost in thought, holding the cloth to her own face.

Sidney touches Marty's chin and looks into her face. She shines her phone light into Marty's eyes.

SIDNEY   Pupils are okay. Bones intact. Better go to the hospital to be sure no concussion, though.

Marty moves out of Sidney's grasp.

MARTY   No.

Sidney looks at her, questioning. Then looks straight ahead.

INT. HOTEL—HALLWAY—NIGHT

A HOTEL WORKER knocks on the door of ROOM 505.

Sidney opens the door to receive a FIRST AID KIT. Sidney hands the worker a 500-peso bill.

INT. HOTEL—MARTY'S ROOM—NIGHT

Sidney tends to Marty's wounds. She examines the bruises and cuts on her face.

They're mid-catch-up. Sidney notices a box of cigarettes resting near the TV.

SIDNEY   You changed to lights.

MARTY   Wanna steal them when I'm not looking?

Sidney ignores the old reference.

MARTY   I only smoke one a day now, anyway. Don't want to end up in—what hospital do you work at?

SIDNEY   Philippine General. PGH turned out to be a good choice. Budget-wise. And—because we're in the kind of country

	we're in—we see a lot of injuries that we don't see in the States.
MARTY	Like these injuries?
SIDNEY	Nah. This is just mild, FilAm mess.
MARTY	Brock's moving up in the world.
SIDNEY	*[smiles wryly]* And you. Where are you in the world these days, weather scientist?
MARTY	Living out of a backpack. Project to project. Tacloban was USAID. Next one will be Guam.

Sidney pauses.

SIDNEY	I'm sorry. I shouldn't have said that back there. Any of that. That was… spiteful.

Marty nods, accepting this. Nodding makes her wince.

SIDNEY	Hold still.
MARTY	How's cousin Jing?
SIDNEY	She's like you. Living to fight another day. You didn't see her reporting in Tacloban?
MARTY	We went a little later. Fewer cameras.
SIDNEY	That must have been… something.
MARTY	Yeah, it…

Her eyes get distant.

SIDNEY	*[gentle]* Hey.
MARTY	*[abrupt]* You still in Teachers' Village?
SIDNEY	I outgrew Jing's spare room. Leah and I have a condo on Taft. In Manila.

Sidney finishes dressing Marty's wound.

SIDNEY	There. How's the pain? One to ten?

Marty is quiet. She looks away. Sidney turns her back to Marty and packs up the first aid kit.

SIDNEY   I'll leave you some gauze—

MARTY   Thirteen.

Sidney is alarmed.

SIDNEY   Jesus, Marty, if that's the case, we should get you to the—

MARTY   That's how many. Since you. Mostly women. A dude and, a genderqueer, person in there too.

Sidney drops the kit and picks up her own stuff.

SIDNEY   Good night, Marty. Thanks for the scorecard.

MARTY   And with every single one of them, I kept looking for you.

Sidney freezes. Marty gets emotional.

MARTY   I needed to see you. I thought—I thought back then, not telling you everything about, about what I was going through—I thought I was protecting you. Or me. And now I have to—however many times. With however many more people. I have to live with that again and again.

SIDNEY   You don't have to blame yourself. And you weren't the only one.

MARTY   I know I—

SIDNEY   No, even though I was the one who, who left— There was a, a you-shaped absence. For months.

Sidney stops herself.

SIDNEY   I can't do this.

She moves to leave.

MARTY   I told you before not to hate yourself. For anything that happened with me.

SIDNEY   You're not the one—thirteen people? I had zero. I barely had room in me for anyone—for Leah—at first—I can't even believe I—

MARTY	Listen.
SIDNEY	No. You listen. I left you once. Once. You left me so many times. And if I had stayed, you would have never stopped leaving me. Your pain would have always taken, fuckin, precedence. So don't. Telling me this now—you don't do this to someone with my history!
MARTY	*[finally bursting out]* How am I responsible for your history? Mine and yours? How?

Sidney's overcome. She goes silent.

Marty gets up. She wipes her face, wincing. She opens the door for Sidney to go.

Sidney leaves, decisive, confident, and enraged.

Marty closes the door quietly. She leans her head against it and closes her eyes.

A long moment passes.

A knock.

SIDNEY	Martika. Marty, I forgot my phone in there.

Marty sniffs. This is absurd. She sees Sidney's phone near the TV.

She unlocks the door and opens it a crack.

MARTY	Here—

Sidney grabs Marty and kisses her.

INT. HOTEL—MARTY'S ROOM—NIGHT

They're in bed—their sex is intense and desperate, making up for lost time.

INT. HOTEL—MARTY'S ROOM—NIGHT

They're awake, in each other's arms. Holding each other like they used to.

A tear falls down Marty's cheek. Sidney wipes it.

SIDNEY	I should've done everything differently. I didn't know how.
MARTY	I didn't either. I didn't know either.

INT. HOTEL—MARTY'S ROOM—EARLY MORNING

They shower together. It's not as playful as when they were younger, but it's knowing and tender.

They get dressed on opposite sides of the room. They return to their present selves.

INT. HOTEL—MARTY'S ROOM—DAY

Sidney and Marty sit next to each other on the bed.

MARTY	Look. You don't owe me anything—
SIDNEY	Martika.

She takes Marty's hand. She kisses her palm.

MARTY	Can we, maybe, agree on something?

Sidney waits.

MARTY	If you write to me, I'll answer as soon as I get it. Even if it's just to say, I don't know what to say.
SIDNEY	And if you write to me, yeah. I think that's a better system than silence.

Marty nods. Sidney stands and gets emotional again.

SIDNEY	Marty, I—

Sidney still can't say she loves Marty.

MARTY	It's okay.

They kiss goodbye. Sidney leaves. Marty inhales and exhales, alone in the room.

MGA LIHAM (THE LETTERS) 2013–2016

A BLANK SCREEN. The sound of wind and waves.

MARTY [VOICEOVER]   Dear Sid...

We see Marty with a YOUNG ASSISTANT setting up equipment on a windy coastal area; it could be the California coast or a severe island.

MARTY [V.O.]	With each gig, I find out more about what I'm gonna be. The word for me lately is "experimentalist."

Marty wakes up in a hotel from a nightmare.

MARTY [v.o.]   I have to stay outside. I work with the boundary layer of the atmosphere. The layer we're all in. The one we influence. The one we're responsible for.

Sidney passes Leah in the hallway of the Philippine General Hospital. They're polite, but Leah's smile is chilly.

MARTY [v.o.]   People keep asking me if I want to be on TV news like a couple of my classmates. I don't. Really! I guess I just… want to be in it, finding out.

Marty's in the library, reading MY SAD REPUBLIC by Eric Gamalinda.

MARTY [v.o.]   How's your Ate? How's med school closing out? What are your dreams lately?

Sidney, Jing, and Nik sit around Jing's table, helping Sidney write a dating profile and laughing.

MARTY   If I don't hear from you, I get it. Just know I wish all the good for you. For all the good that you are.

Sidney studying with her fellow medical students late at night in a crowded dorm.

SIDNEY [v.o.]   Dear Marty…

Sidney visits the National Museum and looks at the 1960s Modern Art exhibit.

SIDNEY [v.o.]   A deal's a deal, no? I could tell you about school. Rounds. Commuting. New people. But I dunno. I just think, overall, I'm making friends with my loneliness.

Sidney dances and gets drunk at a bar's Ladies' Night.

She ends up in bed with a GIRL FROM ABROAD.

SIDNEY [v.o.]   I don't know if that's a good thing.

Sidney lies awake next to the Girl from Abroad.

Sidney sits in a giant test room for the United States Medical Licensing Examination. She and the students open their examination books at the same time and begin.

SIDNEY [v.o.]   Being a doctor can be so weird.

Marty's on a date with SOME GUY. He's warm, kind, and handsome. They walk down a chilly street in the early evening.

SIDNEY [v.o.]   Care is an act of connection. What's more vulnerable and powerful than that? But we have to learn how to distance ourselves.

Marty lies awake next to SOME GUY sleeping.

SIDNEY [v.o.]   I feel like some doctors take it further. Like they become mechanics.

Sidney is back at a neighborhood karinderya. Jing is introducing the condition of an INFORMANT from the community. Sidney examines the patient with a stethoscope and a blood pressure cuff.

SIDNEY [v.o]   Should I learn that too? That distance?

Marty packs her car with camping gear.

SIDNEY [v.o.]   Add this to the lifelong list of questions I would've liked to ask my mom. Maybe that's my dream lately. Just the dream I've always had.

Marty's camping with three other scientists. She refuses a beer. She laughs with them. She's having a good time.

SIDNEY [v.o.]   Jing wrote an exposé about the biggest plastic polluters here. She says corporate crime is harder to report on than governmental crime. But she did it. She always does it. I'm sending the link.

Sidney's at her graduation ceremony in a University of the Philippines sash. Her Filipina family stands to applaud her.

HAROLD VETROMILE, Sidney's white American dad, is there too, looking proud and awkward all at once.

SIDNEY [v.o.]   I think of you too, dear Marty. I hope you're safe and loved where you are. I hope the "it" you're in is a good one.

Marty and her mom share an awkward lunch in California.

MARTY [v.o.]   Do you think it's just our destiny to always be a specific kind of lonely? Maybe it's kind of our power?

Marty gives her mom a hug goodbye. Edna is stiff and doesn't reciprocate.

MARTY [v.o.]   I know however you decide to be, Sid, folks will be lucky
to have your care.

Sidney reads an email: her residency match at a hospital in California.

SIDNEY [v.o.]   The perennial question: stay or go? I've always felt out of
place everywhere. But here in the Philippines…the word
"home" feels the least dishonest.

Jing comes home, hears the news, jumps up and down, and hugs Sidney.

SIDNEY [v.o.]   But what if home can't pay you enough? That feels so
shallow. But it's also real.

Marty sits in a lab, reading Sidney's email.

*Sidney hugs her cousin Jing at the Philippine Airlines departure terminal
parking lot. She doesn't want to let go.*

MARTY [v.o.]   Congrats on your placement in California, Doctor.

From the LAX arrival terminal, Sidney types a response.

SIDNEY [v.o.]   A few hundred miles south from you, yeah?

In her computer lab, Marty smiles.

Mano Po.

I STILL GET THE OCCASIONAL RACIST JABS FROM FRIENDS

I GET ANNOYED AT THIS CONSTANTLY.

Chinoy

chi-noy (plural Chinoys)
1. Chinese Filipino; its own thing.
2. Different from Filipino Culture or Chinese culture.
   a mix of both, for good & bad

When I was growing up, I had a conversation with my family. I was doing things I wanted to do, and they said I should not.

WHY?

The only reason they gave is-

Because we're Chinese.

I'm not allowed to be seen as anything else despite growing up my whole life here.

I have more in common with people here than my own "kind".

*a city in the province of Benguet.

so I'm writing this in English.

I know I shouldn't feel this way. That maybe I should stop feeling at all. Find somewhere else for myself.

This is why it bothers me when people bring up my race.

I don't want to feel what I feel about it.

Between Panels

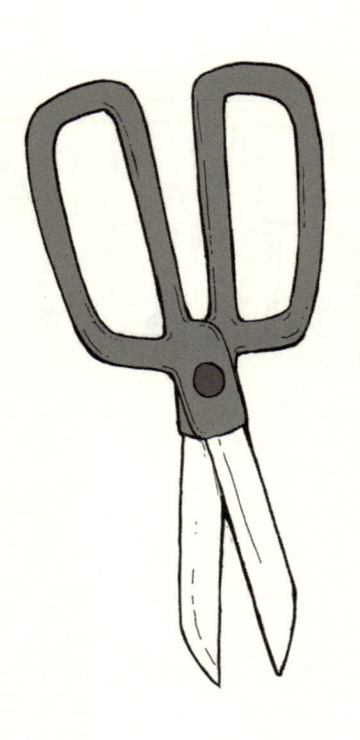

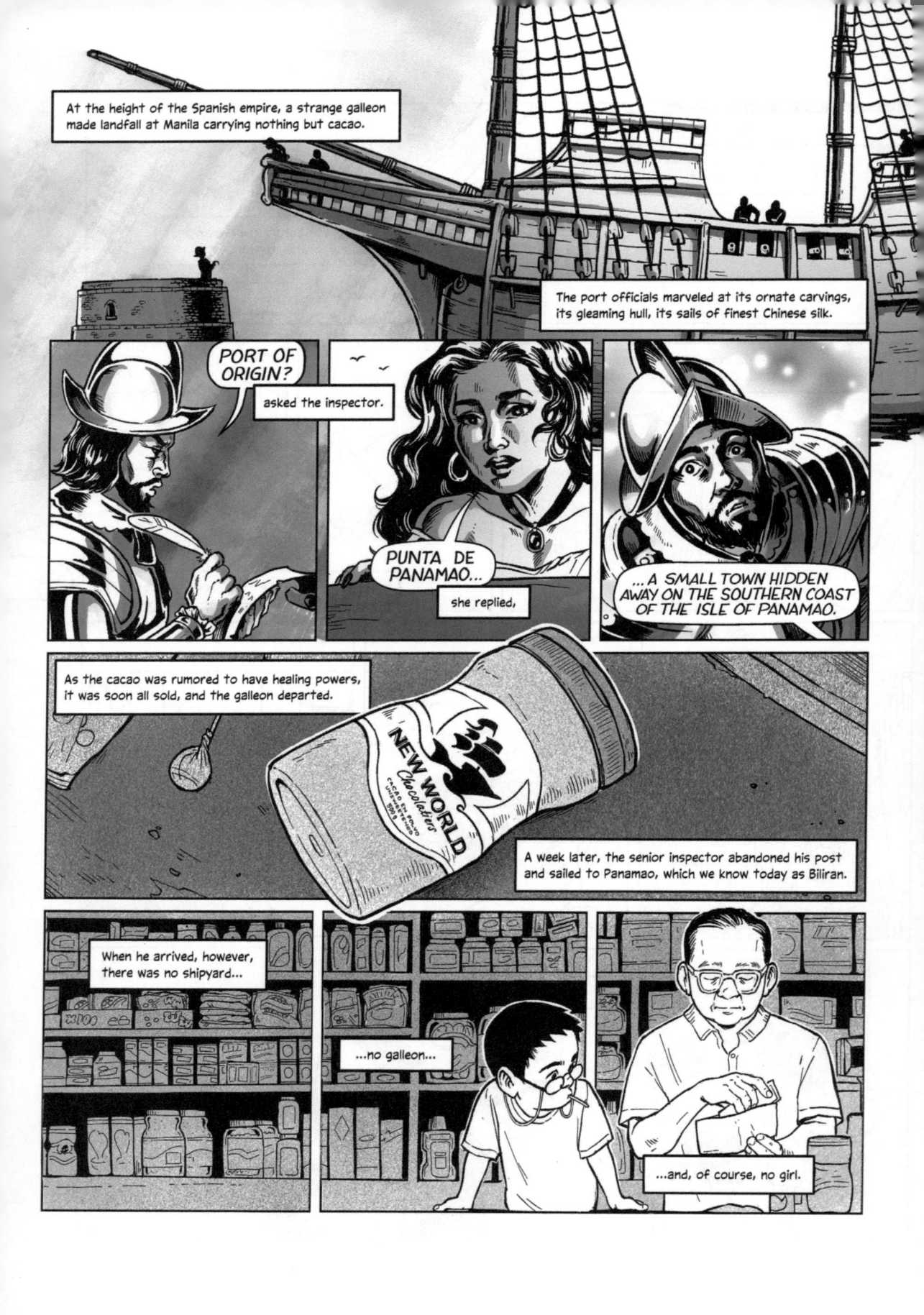

At the time, my favorite comic was *"MISTER LOCK"* by Ray "Pinipig" Pilapil Jr., starring master locksmith Mister Lock and his lackadaisical son, Boy Lakwatsa.

By day, they installed vaults and security systems for the highest bidders. By night, they broke into those very same vaults using secret doors and skeleton keys left behind by the Mister Locks of yesteryear.

See, whenever the comic was getting dry, Pinipig would just do a time jump and refresh the setting...

...from Church treasuries to Commonwealth banks to--in the far future--the crypto-vaults of the landlord of Neo Filipinas.

Every time jump, Boy Lakwatsa becomes the new Mister Lock, whose face (Pinipig once said) was modeled off of world champion boxer Ceferino "Bolo Punch" Garcia's.

That was the name of his signature move:

A feint with the right.

An explosive left hook.

The same move he would have used, bolo knife in hand, to harvest sugarcane back home in Biliran.

Kongkong was born Wen Lin to immigrants from Fujian, China.

In the Japanese years, Intramuros was practically obliterated...

he'd say,

...but Chinatown next door was untouched.

At school in Manila, he went by William, after Shakespeare.

When asked about the war, William only ever told one story...

The kempeitai I met on the street...

...were impressed by my medals from school!

The kempeitai I met on the street...

...were so impressed by my medals from school!

The kempeitai I met on the street...

...were so impressed by my medals from school...

...that when an American fight...

...one that got more and more cinematic with each telling.

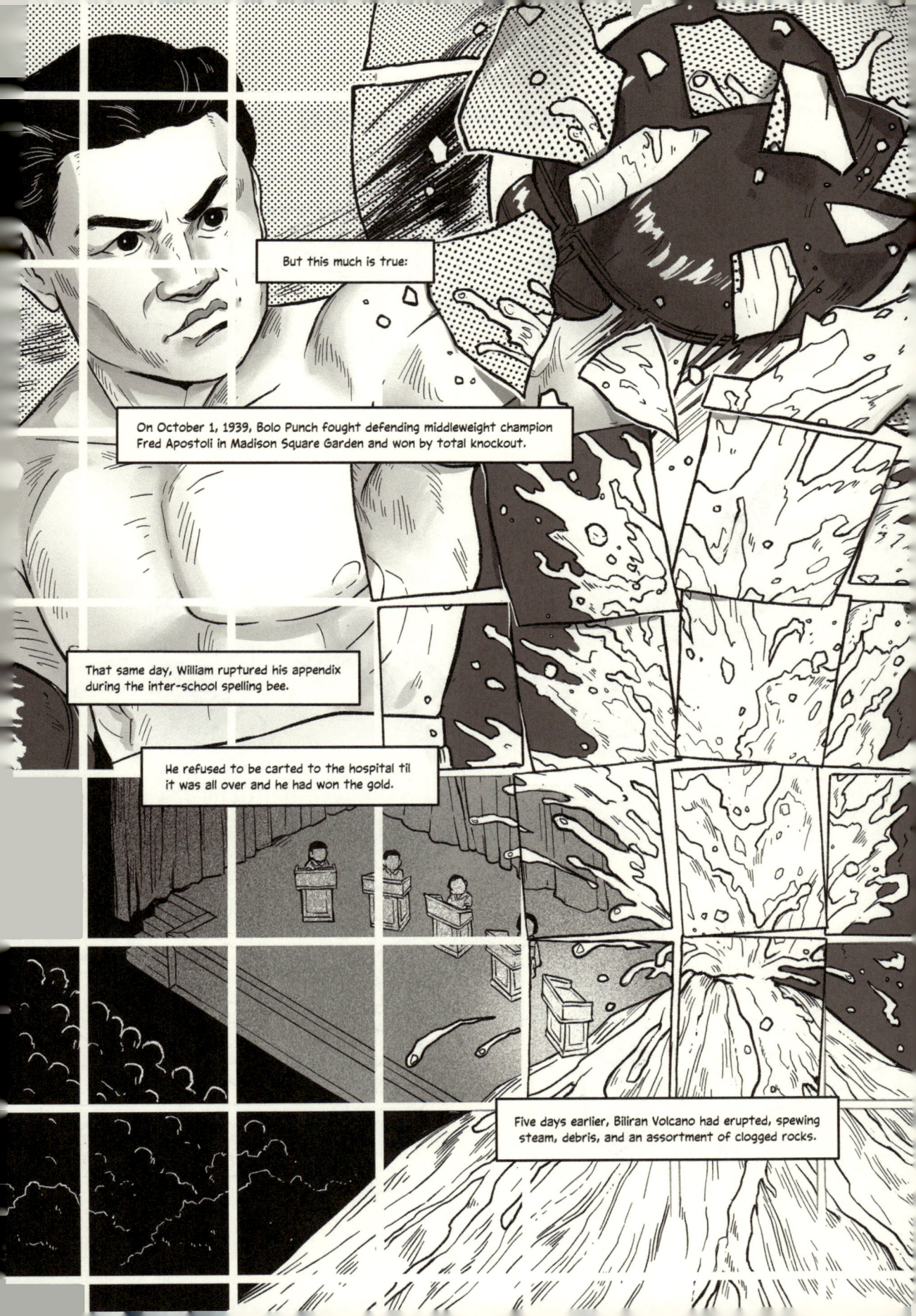

William was hardly picky, but he was picky with his coffee.

GUS PX GOODS

He only drank coffee he made himself, which ruled out Starbucks and the Coffee Bean.

His recipe:

4 tbsp. instant coffee

1 tbsp. creamer

3 tbsp. sugar

and a generous heaping of cacao powder.

Back then, he wouldn't let me sip from his coffee...

...but in exchange would feed me great amounts of "Coffee Crumble"...

...which for some reason came in copper tubs, meaning every time Kongkong pried it open, he would rip the skin off his fingertips again.

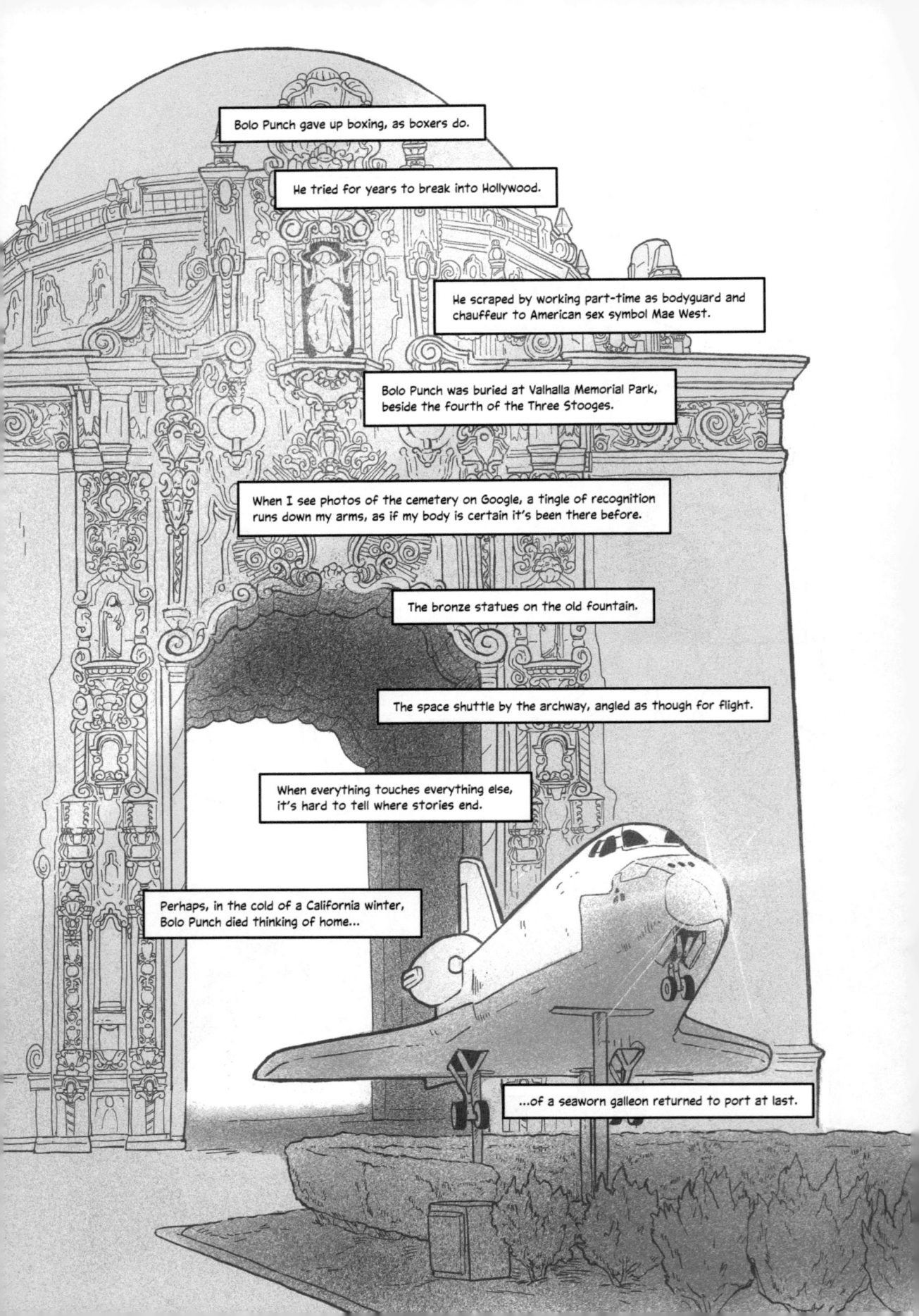

LAUREL FLORES FANTAUZZO

Portraits of Philippine Preservation: Interviews

Cinematic superheroes. Indigenous oral poetry. A physical site of historic exploitation. Photographic evidence of state crimes. A precolonial script. Once-lost literary works. In vibrant, daily ways, the people of the Philippines are engaged in essential acts of preservation, reaching into the past so that its effects live in the present. Conducted by email and messenger apps, here are six conversations with individuals working to preserve aspects of history and culture for generations to come.

Howie Severino (Right) Stands with Student Miguel Martinez (Left), Batangas, 2023, Photograph Courtesy of Howie Severino

A SUBLIME CONNECTION TO THE ANCESTORS: HOWIE SEVERINO AND BAYBAYIN

Howie Severino has been a television journalist for GMA Network in the Philippines for nearly thirty years. He has shot documentaries around the Philippines and around the world, and in recent years, he became fluent in Baybayin.

LAUREL FLORES FANTAUZZO (LFF)   For those who have never encountered it, what is Baybayin?

HOWIE SEVERINO (HS)   Baybayin is the dominant native Filipino script, although at least one leading scholar considers all native scripts in the Philippines Baybayin with regional variations.

LFF   When in your life did you first encounter Baybayin? What did you think of it, then?

HS   I only had vague notions of Baybayin until I investigated a stone slab in Masbate province that had mysterious writing beneath a layer of mud that was cleaned off. An archeologist I was with said it looked like Baybayin. My response was, what's Baybayin? That was about ten years ago.

After my documentary about this stone aired, I got an invitation to talk about Baybayin. I studied it further so I wouldn't feel like a poser and realized the script spoke to me in a soulful way. Today I write every day in Baybayin, and I use it to message friends I've taught it to.

LFF   When did your relationship to Baybayin intensify? Who were your teachers in the language?

HS   I started teaching it informally in 2018–19, but I got serious during the pandemic lockdown when there was little else to do.

I'm self-taught, but I've consulted experts about its history and variations. To be honest, learning to read and write in it is not so hard.

LFF   There have been many turbulent and painful moments in the present-day Philippines. Why focus on Baybayin now?

HS   It makes me feel whole and clear about myself in an increasingly confusing and anxious time. Baybayin has made my native language more logical. I'm a calmer and more confident person because of Baybayin.

LFF   What surprises you about Baybayin and its place in the past and present?

HS   What surprised me is how elegant and logical it is and how much it resonates with people, especially with anyone with Filipino blood or associated with Filipinos.

LFF   How have you seen that resonance manifest in people?

HS   Novelist Gina Apostol and I spent several hours together in Honolulu talking about Filipinos in Hawai'i, Rizal's love life, the murder of Juan Luna's wife Paz, Pinoy food in the US, Gina's hometown, etc. But what did she eventually post about (on Instagram) with such wonder? Baybayin. Only.

She's not unique.

During the pandemic lockdown, the Filipino student organization at Carnegie Mellon University in the US asked me to give a Zoom talk on Baybayin.

Some weeks after the talk, I received a colorful t-shirt with "Carnegie Mellon" rendered in Baybayin. It was their new org shirt. Someone in their org had also created her own Baybayin font. A father of one of the students messaged me to say he and his son were now messaging each other in Baybayin as their private code; the father was part of my audience. It has become a new form of bonding between father and son, just as Baybayin has been a way for me to bond with so many others.

In August 2023, one of those Carnegie Mellon students, US-born Miguel Martinez, came to visit me in Batangas. Without planning to, we both wore the org's Baybayin shirt.

LFF   You've been a broadcast journalist for many years. What relationship does reportage have with the act of preserving a Philippine script?

HS   It's easier to establish rapport since Baybayin is like motherhood. It breaks the ice, especially if someone sees their name in Baybayin for the first time. The joy I see in their faces gives me joy. By then, I can ask them anything.

LFF   Can you say more about Baybayin resembling motherhood? Do newcomers to the script somehow recognize Baybayin as a maternal language?

HS   It's like motherhood because its nobility is generally accepted; it's often an object of love.

LFF   What other encounters have you had with folks who encounter, or reencounter, Baybayin through you?

HS   Everything from skepticism to curiosity to epiphany. For some, Baybayin has been life-changing.

I know people who have devoted their careers to Baybayin. Those who know and practice it form a community of people who generally value heritage and language.

It's a form of expression that's aesthetically and emotionally pleasing and draws people to be creative.

At the same time, those who champion it are exasperated by the government's shallow interest and shoddy use of it, even in a token way.

LFF   How is Baybayin used now in an institutional way in the Philippines, if at all? What do you dream of for its use?

HS   Baybayin is used as a design element or as a nod toward indigenous identity without any wide understanding of what is written. Not many know that it was in Philippine currency or on Philippine passports. It's on government buildings.

My dream? That it be taught to all students in the Philippines, and that Filipinos toggle on their phones between Latin and Baybayin keyboards.

While I await that faraway dream, I'm quite happy to possess a form of knowledge that connects me in a sublime way to my ancestors.

LFF   Do you have a favorite phrase in Baybayin that you can share with us?

ᜊᜄᜒᜈ᜔, ᜊᜓᜆᜒᜈ᜔, ᜈᜒᜈᜓᜈᜓ

Maging mabuting ninuno—Be a Good Ancestor

Janna Añonuevo Langholz, Saint Louis, 2022, Photograph Courtesy of Janna Añonuevo Langholz

RESISTING THE COLONIAL PROJECT: JANNA AÑONUEVO LANGHOLTZ AND THE 1904 WORLD'S FAIR

Interdisciplinary artist Janna Añonuevo Langholtz works across genres, including photography, performance, and relational art. She is the founder of the Filipino American Artist Directory and the independent caretaker of the site of the Philippine Village at the 1904 World's Fair.

LFF You were born in proximity to the site of the 1904 St. Louis World's Fair in Missouri, where white Americans placed Indigenous Filipinos on display in dehumanizing ways. What are your earliest memories, being of Philippine descent in contemporary St. Louis?

JANNA AÑONUEVO LANGHOLTZ (JAL) I didn't have any awareness of being of Philippine descent until I was much older. Growing up in St. Louis, I was often misidentified as Native American, but I don't remember anyone ever asking me if I was Filipino. I was featured on the evening news once when I was in elementary school, dressed as a Native American, because my teacher asked me to as part of a class assignment on Thanksgiving traditions. I didn't know any better, and no one questioned it at the time, either in the early 1990s or later. I liked reading the Laura Ingalls Wilder series and often wore my hair in braids because I identified with her as a young girl, and at the time I didn't know I looked any different than my white classmates.

I also remember when my Girl Scout troop leader had to fill out a demographics form during a camping trip, and she had marked one girl as a Pacific Islander. I looked around at the other girls and couldn't figure out who they could be. When I asked, the troop leader gave me a funny look and said, "That's you."

Looking back on it now, I had a lot of similar moments of misrecognition or confusion in childhood, and there are probably others that I've forgotten by now. I didn't have any Filipino friends, teachers, or family in St. Louis other than my mom, and I didn't meet my family in the Philippines until I was eighteen. The 1904 World's Fair has been a long-enduring interest, and when you grow up in St. Louis, I think that history can encompass you without even knowing it.

LFF When did you first become aware of the physical site of the World's Fair at your birthplace? How did your relationship with that fact develop over time?

JAL I think it's a fact I've always known, but that didn't become fully apparent to me until after I had completed grad school in Dallas. It was 2016, and what made the most sense to me at the time was to move back to the location where I was born and explore my relationship to my hometown. I knew that the site of the 1904 World's Fair still held tremendous historical significance, but that certain aspects like the Philippine Village had never been addressed in a way that I needed them to be. I figured I was going to have to be the person to do that if it was ever going to happen.

At first, I felt a lot of anger that no one seemed to remember or care about the Philippine Village. When I learned about the Indigenous people who died here and that they had never been honored, it shook me to my core in a way that nothing else ever has. Living here on site has been an exercise in finding peace within a historically traumatic place, and that has been part of the healing for me. At present, I feel like I am able to live alongside that history rather than separate from it, and that is where I feel most at home.

LFF   Can you describe a typical day of historical caretaking in St. Louis? What does your routine look like?

JAL   I don't really have a daily routine, but more of a set of responsibilities I've given myself that I regularly carry out. When I established the Philippine Village Historical Site, I designated myself as the caretaker because I didn't know what to call myself, and I didn't have any other power at the present-day site except to care. There is nothing physical to care for, so I consider my work to be for the memory of the place and the people that lived here. Part of how I honor their memories has been walking around my neighborhood with a temporary sign, as well as inviting neighbors and visitors to carry it with me. I've given almost 100 guided walks of the Philippine Village Historical Site since 2021. I also regularly visit the cemeteries where Indigenous people from the Philippines who died during the 1904 World's Fair are buried to bring them fresh flowers.

I think another important part of caretaking for me is spiritual. I maintain residence at the site of the Philippine Village to care for the memories of people who resided here so that they will always be remembered, honored, and never forgotten. In a way, I consider my house to be an altar to them because they lived here too. The past affects the present, but I think the present also affects the past. When I think about it that way, it helps me to reframe the site in a more positive way that merges both.

LFF   Your biography mentions that you have "unrecognized ancestral contributions in museum collections across the United States." Can you say more about that? What tensions exist between your grassroots work and the work of American museum institutions?

JAL   When I started doing research about the exhibits shown in the Philippine Village during the 1904 World's Fair, I came across names of several of my ancestors who contributed items to the Horticulture, Agriculture, Forestry, Fish and Game, and Liberal Arts displays. In addition to the anthropological villages, there were also thousands of Philippine exports exhibited, like our natural resources, to attract American businesspeople to invest in the new colony. After the fair, these items were distributed among three main US museums: the Field Museum in Chicago, the Penn Museum in Philadelphia, and the Smithsonian in Washington, DC.

My ancestors that I know of have traditionally been landowners, farmers, fishermen, and folk healers, so it makes sense that their contributions ranged from lumber, native plants with ceremonial and medicinal uses, rice farming and fishing equipment, and practical, everyday items like brooms. One entry that I found most interesting was for a model house that was likely built and given to World's Fair agents by a great-great-lolo. It probably still exists in a museum collection somewhere, but because these objects were so poorly attributed and labeled, I might not ever know exactly which one it was.

I've frequently encountered tension between the work I'm doing and the institutions that now control these histories, objects, and human remains. I think the colonial project relies on forgetting and the erasure of identity, and now, after so many generations, these institutions assert complete ownership over ancestral inheritances when you cannot prove they belong to you. In my opinion, it was designed that way to make it as difficult as possible for descendants to reclaim everything that belongs to us. Because if it were easy, we would all remember, and these institutions would no longer be able to control our narratives.

LFF   You have visited your family in the Philippines over the years. What region do they hail from? What conversations have you had about your work with them?

JAL   Part of my family hails from Laguna, from a small town in the valley of the Sierra Madre mountains, and has been rooted there for centuries. It's the place I most associate with home in the Philippines. My Añonuevo side is more of a mystery because they were said to be "travelers," and none of my relatives that I've spoken to know where they originated and how they came to our town. When I took a DNA test, several other regions in the Philippines lit up from Central and Northern Luzon, the Visayas, and Mindanao. I've been able to corroborate some of this information with death records dating back to the 1700s. I might not ever know more than that, but it's comforting to me to know that my ancestors had connections to a lot of different places.

During my last trip to the Philippines, I brought printouts of my research to show my family, including the entries I had seen in a 1904 World's Fair catalog and photos of historical objects in museum collections. My uncles, aunts, cousins, mom, and I sat down around a table outside to ponder them. No one remembered the names of those ancestors. My uncles rode their bikes around town to make inquiries on my behalf, but they explained that it might come across as odd to be asking those questions after so long. For them, life is more about day-to-day survival than recalling the past.

I met with a neighbor who is also a distant relative and lives across the street from my family's ancestral house. She shares a last name with one of the ancestors listed in the catalog and thought she might be able to help, so she invited my mom and me over for meryenda. After I showed her the information I had, she said that the last direct descendant of that person likely died many decades ago.

My final effort during the trip was to visit the town cemetery and look for those names. It's not very big, so it took me an afternoon to cover most of it. Although a lot of people in my family's town are descendants of those ancestors in 1904, I could not find their graves, or they were unmarked.

LFF   What are your long-term goals with the site of the 1904 World's Fair and the memory of the Indigenous peoples who lived and died there?

Once the permanent historical marker is placed, I imagine that the site of the Philippine Village will become more self-sustaining since I won't have to carry the sign. I still plan to offer guided walks to people who come to visit and learn about its history. I also plan to soon place grave markers for six of the individuals who are still buried in St. Louis.

A long-term goal that I have is to establish a physical space outside of my own living space where I can properly welcome and host visitors. I would also like it to be a space for community events and to house my growing collection of materials related to the Philippine Village and the 1904 World's Fair.

Overall, I hope my efforts not only raise awareness about the horrific events of the past, but recognize the ongoing struggles still faced by Filipinos and Indigenous people today as a result of the United States' colonization of the Philippines.

Photograph by Raffy Lerma

"Pinapangako ko'ng itago ang inyong mga alaala sa aming puso at isipan. Ipagdadasal ko na makamit natin and hustisya at manatiling malakas para sa ibang mga pamilya ng mga biktima."

"I promise to keep your memory in our hearts and minds. I pray we attain justice and remain strong to help other victims' families." Part of the testimony of one of the widows who, along with other families of drug war victims, gathered to remember their departed loved ones on the eve of All Saint's Day in Quezon City, October 31, 2023.

A COMMITMENT TO BE PRESENT: PHOTOGRAPHER RAFFY LERMA AND STATE VIOLENCE

Raffy Lerma is an award-winning photojournalist. He worked for the *Philippine Daily Inquirer* for over a decade and shifted to independent coverage of the Philippine government's war on drugs.

LFF   How did you come to your vocation as a photojournalist? What are your first personal memories of photography?

RAFFY LERMA (RL)   I always loved looking at photographs when I was a child. We had a collection of books and magazines back then. I remember browsing through the images before reading the text. Images brought me to places. They stirred my curiosity, imagination, and my longing for adventure. Photography showed me a glimpse of other people's lives and their cultures. Other images impacted my life, and I empathized with disaster and conflict victims as you see the humanity, or lack thereof. I knew then, as a child, that photographs were powerful in moving people and a tool for change.

LFF   Have you ever personally experienced encounters with violence, crime, or the police in the Philippines?

RL   I have. One of my earliest encounters was when I was beaten by police and government security personnel back in college. I don't want to go into details anymore.

LFF   I'm sorry. That's awful.

RL   I can say that I was performing my duty as a member of the media when I experienced it.

LFF   In your career since then, you photographed crime, climate disasters, and violence in your time at the *Philippine Daily Inquirer*. What shift did you notice in 2016?

RL   What was evident in 2016 was that violence, or inciting violence, by the state was blatant. The former president showed utter disregard for human rights following the scale of the killings in the drug war.

Though killings were already happening even before 2016, and up to this day, with the current administration of President Marcos Jr., I have never had a president who would openly say killing a person or a group of people was ok. What was more depressing was the support of most of society, who cheered him on. There was a lack of empathy for the victims and their families.

LFF   How did your personal, emotional state change as you witnessed the scale of violence from 2016 to the present? What affected you the most?

RL   I am still processing it to this day. What helped me emotionally through the years was talking about it, getting support from friends and colleagues, and being part of a bigger community of those who responded to the drug war, along with the victims' families.

When you see so much violence, cruelty, indifference, and apathy, it will affect you. It was not a single event but a series of events that were painful to bear.

What for me was the most painful was not the violence itself but, most of all, a society that agreed to the violence and the killing of thousands of Filipinos.

Sa sarili natin bansa pumayag tayo sa pagpatay ng kapwa Pilipino. Yung mali naging tama at yung tama naging mali. In our own country, we agreed to the killing of fellow Filipinos. What was wrong became right, and what was right became wrong.

It was hard to accept this.

LFF   Victims and survivors of vigilante and police violence have looked to journalists on this beat as resources, since there are so few resources available to them otherwise.

RL   I know, and it's hard to call myself a journalist anymore.

LFF   What assistance have you offered, and what relationships have you developed? What has surprised you, if anything?

RL   I am still a photographer and use my photography to tell stories, but I know I have gone beyond my duty as a journalist. I took an active role in the response to the mass killings that happened in the drug war. I knew I could do more to help the victims' families, so I chose to do so and remain with them. This is not a project for me, but a commitment to be present with this community, helping the victims' families search for justice and accountability.

LFF   International and local attention to vigilante and police violence has waned since 2016. How have you and fellow photojournalists continued in your work without that outside interest and support?

RL   Many have moved on. But it is not only because of the lack of local and international interest and support. It also has to do with the psychological trauma of journalists with so much exposure to violence, especially if the state is responsible. It's overwhelming, and you feel helpless from the culture of violence and impunity.

Being a photojournalist alone cannot support my documentation of vigilante and police violence. I have also shifted to documenting the victims' families in their journey of healing, community building, and pursuing justice and accountability. I find work and do other things within human rights advocacy through arts, journalism, activism, and photography to support my documentation. I also collaborate with different advocacy groups.

LFF   Are there any personal anecdotes or memories you can share about why it is important for you to continue this work?

RL   I recently received this message from a victim's family member who lost her father and brother in the drug war back in 2016. She wrote in Tagalog, "If there were a witness to the pain, suffering, struggle, and achievements I have gone through the years, that would be you. Thank you. Because of your pictures, I now understand why I am here and why I need to continue. It's hard, but we need to fight back."

I documented the violence, which serves as a photographic record that these crimes did happen, so that present and future generations remember and learn in the hope that it will not happen again. It's also important to actively use these images to resist the culture of violence and impunity in our society.

LFF   For anyone else who wishes to support victims and survivors of violence in the Philippines, what do you suggest?

RL   Some groups support the victims and survivors of violence in the Philippines. Please consider helping groups like Program Paghilom, Rise Up for Life and for Rights, Solidarity with Orphans and Widows, the Archdiocese of Kalookan, and the Silingan Mothers.

Read up. We cannot just be bystanders anymore. We must get involved and act.

It's easy to say, "Justice for the victims." But to attain justice, we must be willing to help and work hard for it.

TAPESTRIES OF COLLECTIVE MEMORY: JEFFREY SONORA AND FILM PRESERVATION

Jeffrey Sonora is the vice president of FPJ Productions in the Philippines, a film restoration company. He is a member of the Society of Filipino Archivists for Film and the Southeast Asia Pacific Audio Visual Archives Association.

LFF   Tell me about your first encounter with Philippine cinema. When in your life did you see a Filipino movie that was meaningful to you?

JEFFREY SONORA (JS)   My exposure to Philippine cinema began with the rich heritage of my family's involvement in the industry. I was enchanted by its magic from an early age. My great-grandfather was Fernando Poe Sr. He left a lasting legacy on Philippine cinema during the 1930s. He acted, directed, and produced, leaving a mark through iconic works such as *Darna*.

One film that holds a special place in my heart is *Panday*. Set against the vibrant backdrop of the 1980s, a pivotal period in my own coming-of-age journey, *Panday* captured my imagination like few other films had done before. It transported me, weaving together a tapestry of heroes, villains, and enthralling narratives. At its core was the story of Flavio, a humble blacksmith turned hero, whose quest to defend his town from darkness deeply resonated with me.

Panday transcended entertainment; it became an immersive experience that fueled my passion for storytelling and fostered a profound appreciation for the diverse landscapes of Philippine cinema. Through its characters and themes, the film left an impression on me, shaping my understanding of storytelling within the realm of film.

LFF   How did you move into the realm of film preservation professionally?

JS   I was alongside my uncle, Fernando Poe Jr. (FPJ), since I was three months old. He was a distinguished actor and director, and he played a significant role in my life, akin to that of a father figure. In 2004, just before his passing, I was deeply engaged in a collaborative project with him. Our project necessitated access to footage from his earlier films. We encountered considerable difficulties due to the scarcity of archival materials.

The accessibility of these materials posed a consistent challenge, primarily limited to formats like Betacam, VHS, Betamax, and DVDs. More critical formats, such as 60-mm film, remained elusive, leaving us unable to retrieve scenes from certain movies. In discussions with archival institutions, we were disheartened to learn that some films had been irretrievably lost—a realization that deeply affected both my uncle and me. These works held immense value for him, symbolizing years of dedication, creativity, and hard work.

This experience spurred my family's determination to preserve our cinematic heritage. My uncle's decision to archive and protect his works was also influenced by the legacy of our family patriarch. Fernando Poe Sr. had faced a similar tragedy during his career as a producer, when all his films, recorded on nitrate, were destroyed in a fire. The loss of these films was a devastating blow, underscoring the vulnerability of cinematic history and the critical importance of preservation efforts.

In homage to FPJ's memory and with an appreciation for the broader significance of safeguarding our cinematic legacy, I pursued a professional path in film preservation.

LFF   What are some of the material and technological challenges of film preservation in the Philippines?

JS   Film preservation in the Philippines faces significant challenges due to the country's tropical climate. High humidity levels and consistently warm temperatures average around, or beyond, 30 degrees Celsius, or 86 degrees Fahrenheit, throughout the year. These conditions pose a considerable risk to the integrity of film materials, highlighting the critical need for maintaining a stable environment with consistent temperature and humidity levels to ensure their long-term preservation.

In response to these challenges, our initial focus when establishing our archive was to evaluate the storage facilities and develop maintenance protocols. Recognizing the importance of temperature and humidity control, we aimed to create a storage environment that would effectively preserve film materials.

Additionally, when my uncle FPJ passed away, we encountered further hurdles in digitizing our film assets due to the limited availability of film scanners and advanced technological resources at the time. To overcome this obstacle, we improvised a makeshift telesine system, utilizing a projector to display positive films while capturing the images with another camera. This approach allowed us to initiate the digitization process despite the limitations we faced.

I conducted research on the transition from standard definition to high definition and eventually to 4K resolution, which was emerging as the new industry standard during the mid-2000s. Participating in conferences such as the International Broadcasting Convention in Amsterdam provided valuable insights. I explored various options for film restoration, scanning, and color grading.

Despite encountering skepticism and discouragement from some quarters in the Philippines, I remained steadfast to pursue solutions and push the boundaries of what was considered possible. The rapid evolution of the industry, particularly the transition from analog to digital formats, underscored the importance of staying abreast of technological advancements to ensure the preservation of our film materials and the continuation of our cinematic legacy.

LFF   Is there a particular film you went to great lengths to save? Can you tell us about that process?

Preserving films is a vital mission for our company, especially considering that many of our films may have only one copy worldwide. We approach each project with a profound sense of responsibility—it's like a do-or-die situation.

One film that holds particular significance is the recorded wedding of my uncle, FPJ, and my aunt, Susan Roces.

LFF   Alongside your uncle FPJ, your aunt Susan Roces was one of the most prolific actresses in Philippine history; her nickname is the "Queen of Philippine Movies," since she appeared in over a hundred films and television programs. Having a recording of their marriage is historic.

JS   Over time, this piece of cinematic history deteriorated significantly, presenting a formidable challenge for restoration.

Our preservation process is methodical and thorough, starting with a comprehensive physical inspection to assess any damage, splices, or degradation. The film then undergoes ultrasonic cleaning to remove accumulated dust and debris. Once prepared, it is meticulously scanned at the highest achievable resolution.

Depending on the extent of damage, additional restoration techniques may be applied, such as the use of a wet gate system to address scratches or imperfections. Color grading and sound enhancement are also conducted within our facility to maintain quality control and uphold the integrity of the original material.

We also process the film through manual, digital film restoration. That takes thousands of hours, meticulously cleaning each frame of the film.

While the specific steps may vary for each film, we ensure that every production, regardless of its personal or historical significance, is treated with the utmost care and reverence for the enjoyment and appreciation of future generations.

LFF   What film are you most excited to restore?

JS   Currently, we're deeply engaged in the restoration process of two significant films: *Aguila* and *Perlas ng Silangan*. These projects hold immense cultural and historical significance for me, as they feature FPJ in leading roles. *Aguila*, helmed by director Eddie Romero, stands out for its poignant depiction of Filipino identity and resilience, making it an essential piece of our cinematic heritage.

Restoring these films presents its own set of challenges, particularly with regards to the deterioration of the film emulsion over time. Despite these obstacles, I'm excited about the prospect of restoring these gems. Both *Aguila* and *Perlas ng Silangan* not only showcase FPJ's enduring legacy and his impact on Filipino cinema but also provide valuable insights into the societal and cultural landscapes of their respective eras.

Beyond the technical aspects of preservation, the restoration of these films is about ensuring that future generations have the opportunity to experience and appreciate the narratives and themes they embody. By breathing new life into them, we're not only paying homage to the talented individuals behind them but also safeguarding a crucial aspect of our heritage for posterity.

LFF   What else do you hope for with the act of film preservation in the Philippines?

JS   I envision a future for film preservation in the Philippines where every film, regardless of its current condition or format, undergoes restoration, preservation, and becomes accessible to audiences.

A significant hurdle we face is the gap between the visual quality of older films and the high standards set by modern technology. Today, many judge content primarily on its visual clarity rather than its historical or artistic significance. Especially in our era of abundant content consumption, there's a real risk that older films may be overlooked or dismissed, depriving audiences of the chance to appreciate their significance. Limited budgets and challenges in archival processes further complicate our efforts to preserve these cinematic treasures.

Film preservation provides glimpses into past societal structures, norms, and historical documentation of places and events. These films serve as invaluable records of different eras.

Growing up in the 1980s, I felt the disappointment of being unable to revisit childhood favorites due to their unavailability. These films serve as a link to the past, allowing us to relive memories and deepen our understanding of our identity.

Ultimately, preserving Filipino films isn't just about safeguarding cinematic history. It's about preserving our collective memory. It's about ensuring that future generations have access to the diverse tapestry of our cultural heritage, enabling them to learn, appreciate, and connect.

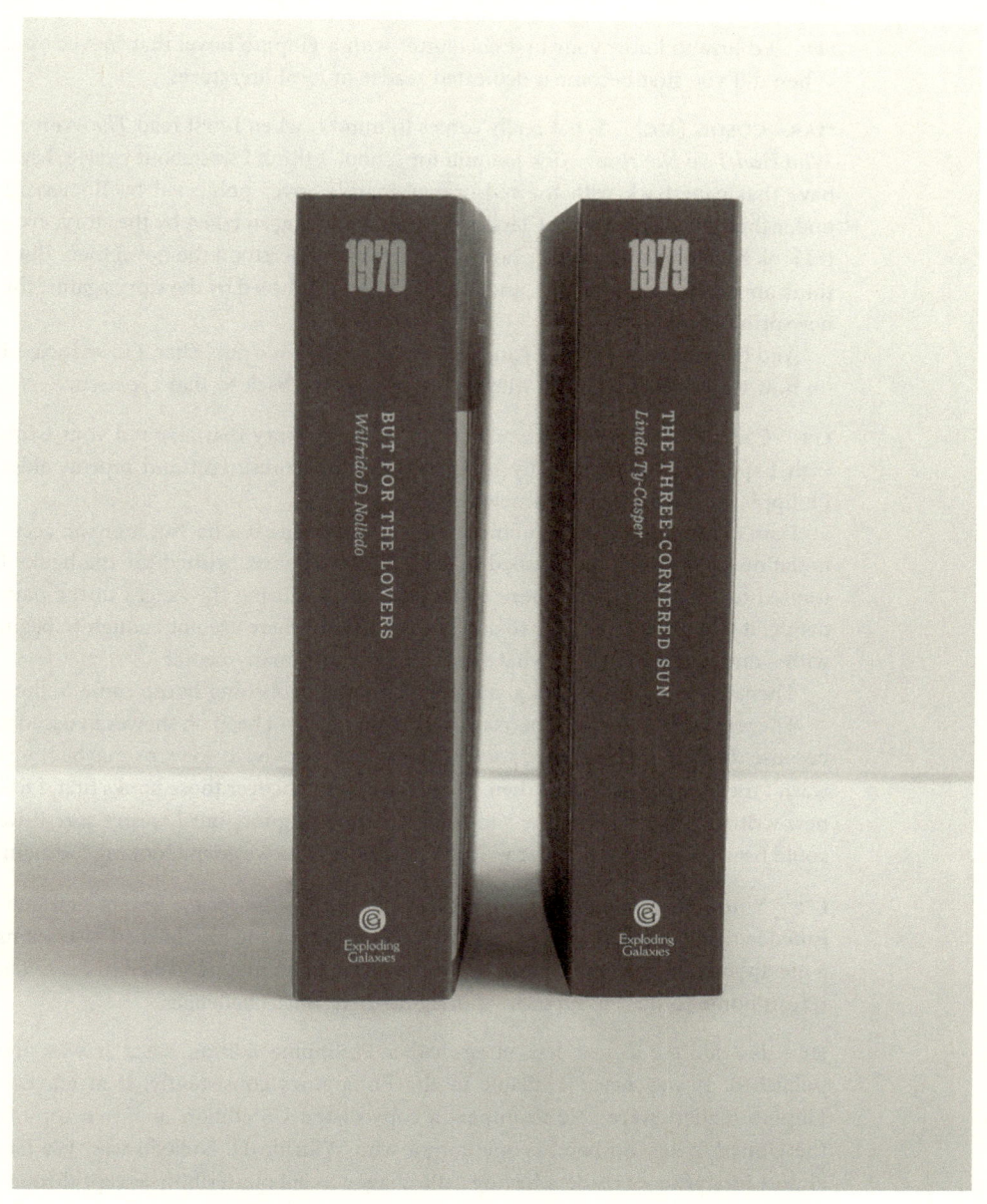

"Exploding Galaxies" First Two Titles, Photograph Courtesy of Mara Coson

Mara Coson is a novelist and a publisher. Her debut novel was *Aliaising* (Book Works, 2018), and she recently founded the press Exploding Galaxies.

LFF   I'd love to know your first encounter with a Filipino novel that moved you. When did you first become a dedicated reader of local literature?

MARA COSON (MC)   What really comes to mind is when I first read *The Woman Who Had Two Navels* by Nick Joaquin for school, I think I was about twelve. I still have that paperback with the red-orange marble cover published by Bookmark under their Filipino Literary Classics. I remember being so taken by the story, even if I look back now and wonder how much I really understood the novel then. But I think about this question now, and I realized I was bothered by the story against the newsprint stock.

And I wonder, as I reply to you, if that may be why, as a publisher, I'm so focused on how the page should feel! Maybe I've been going back to that experience.

LFF   Can you describe a particular moment or memory that inspired your work with Exploding Galaxies? Why have you decided to resurrect and reprint older Philippine novels rather than new work?

I can't pinpoint a precise moment—there was no great a-ha, but more an accumulation of wishes. I had wished to set up a small press, wished for the books I wanted to read to become more easily accessible—during the height of the pandemic, it was near impossible to access libraries and there are not enough to begin with—and wished to share what I was reading with many people.

Then, with a promise and a curious name, the publishing house came to life.

There are too many good books out there that haven't been on shelves in decades because the authors have long gone or their publishers have gone, or maybe it just wasn't the time for the books then. I wanted to help uncover those books first. I feel new writing will always come, and some great writing too, but I wasn't sure if we could hear the urgency of older writings as easily unless we go out looking for them.

LFF   Your inaugural novel was Wilfrido D. Nolledo's *But for the Lovers*, first published in the US in 1970. What was the process by which you republished it? It seems a metaphorical balikbayan, migrant process, for a book first published in the US to return home to the Philippines—I imagine there were challenges.

MC   *But for the Lovers* has never had a Philippine edition since it was first published. It was never available in the Philippines consistently, if at all. Few Filipino readers were able to import a copy of the US edition or buy a copy in the United States. So here, people forgot who Wilfrido D. Nolledo was. We had almost fifty years of readers having little chance to encounter him, except through a short story like "Rice Wine" or just by a name on a list of great writers.

The American publisher of the 1992 edition thankfully understood how important his homecoming was to Philippine literature and reverted the rights to the novel back to the estate. The Nolledos then granted rights to Exploding Galaxies to make this new edition happen. It has been a heartwarming return home for the book, especially for readers experiencing the challenge of his writing for the first time. And that's also where the real challenge is!

LFF Yes. *But for the Lovers* is a hallucinatory novel set during the destruction of World War II in Manila. Exploding Galaxies' second release, Linda Ty-Casper's *The Three-Cornered Sun*, is set in 1896, at the birth of the Philippines' revolution against Spain. How do you see Exploding Galaxies' work in relationship to Philippine history?

MC As Linda Ty-Casper said, "History is our biography, and literature is our autobiography." I think characters in historical fiction especially allow readers empathy to better understand what happened and why they happened through the way things felt right at those moments. In *The Three-Cornered Sun*, instead of cold, hard history, we meet a conflicted family and experience their many motivations and expectations, and disappointments too, as the Philippines came toward independence. With Nolledo's *But for the Lovers*, we sink right into the hot stink of hell along with the characters, and that feeling was as close as the author could take us to the destruction of Manila. Different ways of entering time.

I got asked recently whether publishing the first two books that deal with these big historical moments was intentional or not, and I still am thinking about that. What we hope for is for the books we publish to take us, through fiction, to events that have brought us here, wherever here is. The books can also be less big and more intimate, like what happens with families or with love.

LFF In the Philippines, media and literary institutions often disappear in disturbing ways. We saw two shutdowns of ABS-CBN, for example, and the recent franchise revocation of CNN Philippines, disappearing a decade's worth of journalism, art, and essays. What do you hope for with Exploding Galaxies' work in preservation?

MC We do our part in finding what's been lost or forgotten in time. As publisher, my prime responsibility is to the books we commit to. We have to make sure that they remain easily accessible for as long as we possibly can, and we have to make sure that they're widely studied in universities as much as they're enjoyed at home. If I can do that, then I do my part, and my best, to keep these authors and titles remembered and protected. I'm just at year one of what I hope will be a life's work, so we'll really have to see.

LFF What do you want to see more of, for readers in the Philippines?

MC More books, more shelves, more libraries, more bookstores—more opportunities for publishing, for being heard, for being read, for being studied.

Dorian S. Merina, Sabtang, 2024, Photograph Courtesy of Dorian S. Merina

FROM THE VOICE OF THE MIGHTY SEA CURRENTS: DORIAN MERINA AND LAJI

Dorian Merina is a poet, author, journalist, and teacher. He is the author of *Di Achichuk: Poems and Images from Batanes* (Ateneo University Press, 2019), two chapbooks of poetry, *The Changegiver* and *Stone of the Fish*, and a spoken word album, *Heaven is a Second Language*.

LFF   Batanes is the northernmost province of the Philippines, a group of islands closer to Taiwan than to the most populated island of Luzon. Can you describe your relationship to Batanes? What are your earliest memories of relating to the province and Ivatan traditions?

DORIAN MERINA (DM)   Although I have lived in Batanes, on and off, for more than two decades now, I was born in Los Angeles and spent my childhood mostly in California. It wasn't until I was older that I recognized and was grateful for how hard my grandparents worked to ensure that those of us raised away from Batanes were aware of our connection to this place. They told stories, they cooked the food and maintained the traditions, and hosted relatives from Batanes in their California home. That's why even when growing up, when I was much more interested in MTV, hip-hop, or playing soccer than any notion of "ancestral roots," Batanes was never too far away and was even a constant presence. And that's why, when I first started returning here regularly, it felt familiar. My father had been back. My older cousins had returned. And much of our family still lived here. Though World War II had dislodged my branch of the family from Batanes, most of my father's family stayed here. They're farmers and fisherfolk, and most still maintain that way of life today.

That said, since moving back full-time, which was in 2017, I have had to relearn the most basic Ivatan skills: how to do traditional roofing, how to grow root crops, fish, and harvest from the ocean, and how to relate to my community and express concepts in our traditional language. And I'm still learning! I always keep in mind the name we have for ourselves, Ivatan. Like other tribal peoples, it is intimately related to our place: Ivatan means one who is from Vatan, or this specific island group in this part of the world. We are inseparable from the land, and that is what makes us unique.

LFF   What is Laji, and what is its role in Ivatan culture?

DM   Laji is the traditional oral poetry of the Ivatan people. Its origins predate the arrival of the Spanish in the eighteenth century. It's a social and collective art form traditionally performed in a group setting, such as at a pre-wedding ceremony, called a *kayun*, or a wake for the deceased. It uses highly symbolic or metaphorical language and can play with tone to sound mournful, dramatic, or ironic. It is also place-specific, so a certain Laji singer can be known for a particular melody based on their hometown or include local place names as part of their lyrics.

LFF   Do you have a favorite work of Laji, and can you share it with us?

There are so many! And they have such interesting, distinct qualities. But I will share an excerpt of one Laji that I've been currently interested in.

Nu nunuk du tukun, minuhung as kadisi na
ichapungpung diya am yaken u ñilawngan na.
Kapaytalamaran ava su avang di idaúd
ta miyan du inayebngan na, ta miyan du inayebngan na.
Nu itañis ko am nu didiwen ko
ta nu taaw aya u suminbang diyaken,
nu maliliyak a pahung as maheheyet a riyes
u minahey niya diyaken.

The nunuk on the hill shot forth new leaves and twigs
then suddenly all its branches fell, and I under it.
On what is left I cannot watch boats on the sea
for I stand on the side away from the sea.
I weep in my grief;
it was the sea that made me an orphan;
the sad news came to me in the roar of the breakers,
from the voice of the mighty sea currents.

This version comes from singer Catalina Faronilo Hontomin, who lived on the island of Sabtang. Although in one sense it is a simple mourning song, I love the way it uses the imagery of a *nunuk*, which is a kind of tree here in Batanes, to express the emotion of the singer, with the tree's sudden explosion of growth, regeneration, and loss—all while facing the menacing power of the sea, which is a constant force for Ivatans.

LFF You spent most of your life in the US, and you did a Fulbright conducting research on Laji. How did you come to your decision to live on the Batanes island of Sabtang full time with your family?

DM As I've gotten older, my view on time and how it relates to our individual lives has evolved, which I suppose is natural. I have two great-uncles on my father's side who joined the resistance during the 1940s and were executed by Japanese soldiers. They fought in the hills close to where we live today and were barely teenagers when they were killed. We're still living with that loss because that branch of the family has far fewer relatives alive today. Before that, we had a tribal leader, named Aman Dangat, who rebelled against the Spanish, which led to the entire population of our island being exiled for fifty years. That was from the late 1790s into the 1840s. In those days, that's nearly two generations who were prohibited from living in our homelands. My grandfather's role as a guerilla fighter during World War II also took his family, and by extension, myself and his other descendants, away from the islands.

This kind of violence, dislocation, and disruption is, unfortunately, not unusual for tribal communities. And yet, despite all of the hardship and trauma, Ivatans continue to live in Batanes, as we have for generations. We use our language and place names that have come from our ancestors, farm and fish in traditional ways, and participate in our living cultural practices, such as our *yaru*, or work cooperative, to keep our community going. That's not to say we don't confront big changes or challenges today; we definitely do, but we've managed to keep going in the face of all the obstacles.

At the core of this endurance, for me, is our relationship to the land. Our way of life, our way to feed and house our families, stems from our relationship to this place —the mountains and rivers, the forests and pastureland, the ocean. That's a connection that spans many lifetimes and generations. From when I first started visiting Batanes, I felt a strong desire to move here in a more permanent way, but it took many years to make it happen! I realized only much later that coming back was a commitment to strengthen those ties and relationships and to move them forward for the next generation.

LFF Much of Ivatan literary tradition is oral, and you have begun a library of hardcopy books in Sabtang. What does a daily routine look like, as far as preserving Laji and other forms of participation in your indigenous cultural practices?

DM Yes, we started a small, community-based library, called Aklatan Savidug, during the pandemic. It was an effort to create a supportive and creative space for our community to learn, to read, and to preserve our lifeways as Ivatans. It was also a deliberate effort to give our youth a safe place for learning and positive growth in the midst of the steady and seductive rise of digital misinformation and manipulation. We open it to everyone and share materials that enhance our culture, such as plant medicine and fishing, but we also offer just fun and spooky stories, riddles, or how-to books on cooking and carpentry—whatever our community is interested in. Our latest project is to build up our collection of archival materials about local history and make it directly accessible to our community.

In terms of preserving Laji, I'm not sure if this makes sense, but a lot of my current work turns out not to be directly about Laji—at least not at first. Since the art form is so tied to community and language, I see my work to strengthen those aspects as key to Laji's survival.

Another way to put it is that I've worked on preserving Laji for many years now, and I've realized that just having texts of Laji lyrics has limited value if we no longer have the community spaces in which to perform them or the proper language to express them in. So although I have spent time recording Laji, transcribing the lyrics, and interviewing elders about the poetry, I also see as equally important the need to maintain our other traditions and values, whether land stewardship or weaving, so that down the road, Ivatans themselves call for Laji to be sung and feel a need for it to be heard.

LFF What else do you hope for, with the future of Laji?

DM My goal is to help create a community where Laji is seen as a necessary art, an integral part of our life, rather than something to be performed for others or brought out just for festivals, where the beauty it expresses is honored and enjoyed. These days, it's hard to compete with a karaoke session or the latest TikTok video for enter-tainment. But we're losing something essential if we allow Laji to vanish. It offers so much more. It embodies a way of thinking, a way of being in this particular place. It's a direct connection to our ancestors, yes, but it's also a flexible art form that invites the next generation to play with it, to learn from it, to innovate something new.

Gina Apostol has written five novels, among them *Insurrecto*, named by Publishers Weekly one of the Ten Best Books of 2018, and her most recent, *La Tercera*, out last May. She has been awarded the Rome Prize, the PEN/ Open Book Award, and two Philippine National Book Awards. She grew up in Tacloban, Leyte, in the Philippines, and lives in New York and western Massachusetts.

Rob Cham is an illustrator, comic creator, creative director, and friend. He is best known for his graphic novels *Light* and *Lost*. You can see more of his work at robcham.com.

Scott Lee Chua is a Chinese-Filipino comic creator. Together with Ethan Chua, he coauthored *Doorkeeper*, one of CNN Philippines' Top 10 Comics of 2017. His creative works have garnered the Gabriel Garcia Marquez Prize for literature in translation, the Nick Joaquin Literary Award for short fiction, and a nomination for the Philippine National Book Awards. Scott would like to thank Lawrence Ypil, Linda Collins, Myle Yan Tay, Roshan Singh Sambhi, Andrew Kwan, Ethan Chua, ants chua, Dianne Araral, Kristian-Marc James Paul, Shardul Sapkota, Chia Yaim Chong, Laurel Flores Fantauzzo, and the *Mānoa Journal* editors and team. Mabuhay kayo! Mabuhay ang komiks!

Conchitina Cruz is a professor at the Department of English and Comparative Literature, University of the Philippines Diliman. She received her Ph.D. in English from the State University of New York (SUNY), Albany. Her books of poetry include *Dark Hours* (winner of the National Book Award for Poetry in the Philippines), *elsewhere held and lingered*, *There Is No Emergency*, and *Modus*. She is also the author of *Partial Views: On the Essay as a Genre in Philippine Literary Production*.

Rachelle Cruz is the author of *God's Will for Monsters*, which won an American Book Award in 2018 and the 2016 Hillary Gravendyk Regional Poetry Prize. She coedited *Kuwento: Lost Things, an Anthology of Philippine Myths*, with Lis P. Sipin-Gabon. The second edition of her comics text resource, *Experiencing Comics: An Introduction to Reading, Discussing and Creating Comics*, was published in 2021. Her work has also appeared in

Strange Horizons, Poets & Writers Magazine, the San Francisco Chronicle, and *Yellow Medicine Review,* among others.

Tammy David is a Manila-born photographer and content strategist with a background in documentary photography. Her work has appeared in publications such as the *Wall Street Journal, Foreign Policy, Monocle, Buzzfeed, Financial Times,* and local editions of *Esquire* and *Town and Country.* David's photography has been exhibited in Manila, Singapore, Kuala Lumpur, Hanoi, Jakarta, Seoul, Hamburg, London, and Dubai. Holding diplomas in photojournalism (2008) and multimedia journalism (2014) from the Konrad Adenauer Asian Center for Journalism, her personal work delves into internet culture, fandom, identity, body image, and global perceptions of beauty. David is currently based in New York.

Noelle Q. de Jesus was born in the United States, grew up in the Philippines, and has lived in Singapore for nearly twenty-five years. She is the author of two short story collections, most recently *Cursed and Other Stories* (Penguin Random House SEA), and is currently working on a novel. Her first book of short fiction, *Blood Collected Stories,* won an award and was translated into French. Her English translation of Ricky Lee's first novel, *For B or How Love Devastates Four out of Every Five of Us* came out in May 2023. She has an MFA in fiction from Bowling Green State University, and last year, she was a Fellow at the University of Iowa's International Writing Residency, sponsored by Singapore's National Arts Council. She is a freelance copywriter and editor, a wife, and a mother of two.

Glenn Diaz is the author of the novels *The Quiet Ones* (2017) and *Yñiga* (2022), recipients of the Philippine National Book Award, and *When the World Ended I Was Thinking about the Forest* (2022), published by Paper Trail Projects. Born and raised in Manila, he holds a Ph.D. from the University of Adelaide and currently teaches with the Department of English and Comparative Literature at the University of the Philippines Diliman.

Laurel Flores Fantauzzo is the author of the young adult novel *My Heart Underwater* (Harper 2020) and the nonfiction book *The First Impulse* (Anvil 2017). Their essays have appeared in *CNN Philippines, the New York Times,* and *The Baffler,* and they have been named a Philippine National Book Award finalist, a PEN/FUSION Emerging Writers Prize finalist, and a grantee of the Astraea Lesbian Foundation for Justice.

Ren Galeno is a visual artist from Davao City, Philippines. She graduated Magna Cum Laude from the University of the Philippines Diliman with a degree in Fine Arts and currently works in comics and illustration. She illustrated the 2024 Pulitzer Prize finalist *Searching for Maura* for the *Washington Post.* The work has also received a Gold Medal in Illustrated Reporting from the Society of News and Design. Her first book, *Sa Wala,* was published in 2023. Ren would like to thank her friends, Scott, and the *Mānoa Journal* team! Mabuhay ang komiks!

Eric Gamalinda was born and raised in Manila and currently lives in New York City, where he teaches at the Center for the Study of Ethnicity and Race at Columbia University. "Radio Kiss Kiss" is excerpted from his novel in progress, *Ala-ala at Guniguni* (Memory and Hallucination). The novel, envisioned as a generational diptych, opens with the main character, Del, in her preteens, as she experiences heartbreak and heroism before and during the Japanese Occupation of the Second World War. The second half picks up Del's story thirty years later, during the tumultuous dawn of the Marcos era, as seen through the eyes of her ten-year-old son, who learns of the surprising turns her life took shortly after the war.

Vernadette Vicuña Gonzalez is a professor of ethnic studies at the University of California, Berkeley. She is the author of *Securing Paradise: Tourism and Militarism in Hawai'i and the Philippines* (2013) and *Empire's Mistress, Starring Isabel Rosario Cooper* (2021). She is coeditor of *Detours: A Decolonial Guide to Hawai'i* (2019) and *Bangtan Remixed: A Critical BTS Reader* (2024).

Raffy Lerma is a freelance photographer based in Manila, Philippines. He began his career in photojournalism as a student of the College of Fine Arts at the University of the Philippines Diliman, covering events and street protests that led to the ouster of former President Joseph Estrada in 2001. He worked as a staff photographer for the Philippine Collegian, the university's official student publication, and later served as its photo editor in 2004. Lerma finished his Diploma in Photojournalism at the Konrad Adenauer Asian Center for Journalism at the Ateneo de Manila University. For twelve years, Lerma worked as a staff photographer for the Philippine Daily Inquirer, covering the daily news beat in Metro Manila. He shifted to working independently to focus on his documentation of the Philippines' war on drugs. Lerma has been exhibiting his photographs and giving talks in different parts of the Philippines and the world to help disseminate to a broader audience the realities of the drug war in the country.

Dorian S. Merina is the author of *Di Achichúk: Poems and Images from Batanes*, two chapbooks of poetry, *The Changegiver* and *Stone of the Fish*, and a spoken word album, *Heaven is a Second Language*. He teaches media studies at the University of the Philippines, Diliman, and lives on the island of Sabtang, where he helps run a village library, Aklatan Savidug, and preserve the local indigenous oral poetry, called Laji. More can be found at ivatanlaji.com.

Nita Noveno is the recipient of the 2024 Women's Prose Prize from Red Hen Press, and her hybrid memoir *Mud on the Moon* is set to be published in fall 2026. She teaches composition and literature at the Borough of Manhattan Community College, City University of New York. A graduate of the MFA Creative Writing Program at The New School, Nita is also the founder and host emeritus of Sunday Salon, a long-running reading series in New York City. Her work has appeared in *Identity Theory, Brink, Hippocampus, The Hunger,* and the Asian American Writers' Workshop's *Open City* and *The Margins,* among other publications. Nita grew up in the temperate rainforest of Southeast Alaska and now calls Queens, NY, home.

Jasmine Nikki "Nikay" C. Paredes was born and raised in Cebu City, Philippines. She is the author of two poetry chapbooks, *Reclamations* (Vagabond Press, 2017) and *We Will See the Scatter* (dancing girl press, 2014). She is the recipient of a Loyola Schools Award for the Arts, the Maningning Miclat Poetry Prize, and fellowships from the Ateneo Heights Writers Workshop, the Iligan National Writers Workshop, and the Silliman University National Writers Workshop. Along with Paolo Tiausas, she is the cofounding editor of *TLDTD* (tldtd.org), a biannual journal for Filipino poets and poetry, and a recipient of the 2021 Hawker Prize for Southeast Asian Poetry. In 2016, she immigrated to the United States. She currently resides in Queens, NY, and works as a literary arts administrator.

Michelle Peñaloza is the author of *All The Words I Can Remember Are Poems,* winner of the 2024 Lexi Rudnitsky Editor's Choice Award and the James Laughlin Award, which is awarded by The Academy of American Poets to recognize and support a second book of poetry forthcoming in the next calendar year (Persea Books, 2025). She is also the author of *Former Possessions of the Spanish Empire,* winner of the 2018 Hillary Gravendyk National Poetry Prize (Inlandia Books, 2019), and two chapbooks, *landscape/heartbreak* (Two Sylvias, 2015), and *Last Night I Dreamt of Volcanoes* (Organic Weapon Arts, 2015). Michelle was born in the suburbs of Detroit, MI and raised in Nashville, TN. She now lives in Covelo, California.

Martin San Diego is an independent documentary photographer from the Philippines. He photographs the different manifestations of resistance. Through his work, he questions histories and ideologies pervaded by his country's colonizers. Martin regularly works for *The Washington Post* on stories in the Philippines and with various United Nations agencies for campaigns in and outside the country. He is a multiple grantee of the National Geographic Society, a finalist of The Aftermath Project Grants, and an alumnus of the Angkor Photo Festival Workshops. His work has been published on *VICE News, The Guardian, Al Jazeera, The Telegraph,* and locally on *Rappler.* He graduated with a degree in computer science from De La Salle University in Manila in 2013. Martin pursued his childhood dream of journalism after leaving corporate life and juggling various lens-based work. In 2018, he finished Visual Journalism at the Ateneo de Manila University as a fellow of the Konrad Adanauer Stiftung Media Programme Asia. In the course of the program, his love for long-form storytelling and photo documentaries was developed. When not at work, Martin is probably on his bike, chasing sunsets.

R. A. Villanueva is the author of *A Holy Dread*, winner of the 2024 Alice James Award, and *Reliquaria*, winner of the Prairie Schooner Book Prize (University of Nebraska Press, 2014). His new work has been featured by the Academy of American Poets and National Public Radio, and his writing appears widely in international publications such as *Poetry London* and *The Poetry Review*. His honors include commendations from the Forward Prizes and fellowships from the Sewanee Writers' Conference, the Constance Saltonstall Foundation for the Arts, and Kundiman. Born in New Jersey, he lives in Brooklyn.

PERMISSIONS

Grateful acknowledgment is made to all the authors, translators, and copyright holders for permission to publish their work. Reprints are not permitted without their written consent. The editors thank the following for permission to reprint previously published works:

Noelle Q. de Jesus, who wrote the short story "Michael," which was one of the thirteen stories comprising *Cursed and Other Stories*. Printed by permission of Penguin Random House Southeast Asia, 2019.

Nikay Paredes wrote the poem "We're Always Thinking about Our Dead," which was first published as a limited-edition broadside designed by John Candell for the Red Door Series, presented by St. Mark's Episcopal Church in Jackson Heights, NY.